07/30/08

P9-AQK-496

Fighting the AIDS and HIV Epidemic
A Global Battle

Fighting the AIDS and HIV Epidemic
A Global Battle

ISSUES IN FOCUS TODAY

Maurene J. Hinds

 Enslow Publishers, Inc.
40 Industrial Road
Box 398
Berkeley Heights, NJ 07922
USA

http://www.enslow.com

Library of Congress Cataloging-in-Publication Data

Hinds, Maurene J.
     Fighting the AIDS and HIV epidemic : a global battle / Maurene J. Hinds.
        p. cm. — (Issues in focus today)
     Includes bibliographical references and index.
     ISBN-13: 978-0-7660-2683-4
     ISBN-10: 0-7660-2683-3
     1. AIDS (Disease)—Juvenile literature. 2. HIV infections—Juvenile literature.
  I. Title.
     RC606.65.H56 2008
     614.5'99392—dc22

                                                          2006030194

Printed in the United States of America

10 9 8 7 6 5 4 3 2 1

To Our Readers: We have done our best to make sure that all Internet addresses in this book
were active and appropriate when we went to press. However, the author and publisher have
no control over and assume no liability for the material available on those Internet sites or on
other Web sites they may link to. Any comments or suggestions can be sent by e-mail to
comments@enslow.com or to the address on the back cover.

Illustration Credits: Libero Ajello, Centers for Disease Control/Public Health Image Library
(CDC/PHIL), pp. 62, 111; AP/Wide World, p. 101; CDC/PHIL, pp. 5, 22, 50; Corel Corp.,
pp. 65, 113; Digital Stock, pp. 5, 42; Everett Collection, pp. 83, 94; Jim Gathany,
CDC/PHIL, pp. 5, 45; Getty Images, p. 7; William Kaplan, CDC/PHIL, pp. 15, 103; Steve
Kraus, CDC/PHIL, pp. 25, 105; Photos.com, pp. 5, 18, 29, 33, 57, 59, 80, 88, 99, 107, 115,
117; Shutterstock, pp. 3, 5, 9, 12, 38, 52, 55, 70, 73, 109; United Nations, pp. 76, 91.

Cover Illustrations: Shutterstock (background and large photo); BananaStock (small photo).

Contents

Acknowledgments

Special thanks to everyone who viewed a version of the manuscript and provided helpful comments and suggestions.

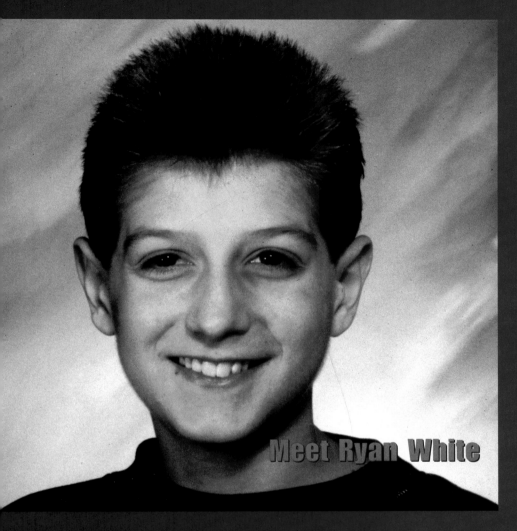

On April 8, 1990, a young man named Ryan White died of AIDS. He was only nineteen years old. His death made national and international news.

White, who lived in Indiana, was a middle-class, white, heterosexual male. He contracted HIV from blood treatments he needed for hemophilia, a clotting disorder. In December of 1984, following surgery, Ryan found out he had HIV infection. He was given six months to live.

When members of his school and community discovered he was HIV positive, they were not supportive. Instead, Ryan and his family faced discrimination and violence. The school expelled him. People threw things at him in public. Someone shot a bullet into his home. After many legal battles, the school allowed Ryan to return if he used a separate bathroom and disposable silverware when he ate lunch. At the time, people did not know much about AIDS. Fears and tensions were high.

After this, Ryan transferred to a school in a nearby town. Here, he was welcomed and lived life as normally as he could. He made national news, and a television movie told his story. He had a new goal in life—to educate people about the facts of HIV and AIDS. He wanted people to know that it is not a "gay" disease, that it cannot be transferred through casual contact, and that it can affect anyone regardless of age, race, gender, or sexual preference. When he died, many people had heard about his fight. Many celebrities attended his funeral, including singers Michael Jackson and Sir Elton John.

In 1990, Congress enacted the Ryan White Comprehensive AIDS Resources Emergency (CARE) Act. At the time, this was the United States' largest federally funded program for the care of those with HIV and AIDS. The act offers health services to those living with HIV/AIDS.

Ryan White will always be remembered as a unique figure in the fight against AIDS. His dedication serves as an inspiration, and, even though the world lost him, his fight led to ongoing health services for many people infected with HIV/AIDS.

What Is AIDS?

What exactly is AIDS? Is it one disease or many? The truth is that AIDS refers to a range of symptoms that result from HIV infection. AIDS stands for *acquired immunodeficiency syndrome*. This disorder is a result of an infection with HIV, which stands for *human immunodeficiency virus*.

What Is a Virus?

Viruses are very simple, parasitic entities. Technically, viruses are not alive, but are like "a brain with no body."[1] This means that they require another life-form in order to duplicate. For viruses, this other life-form is cells. Some viruses cause disease, and some do not. In order for a virus to replicate, it must enter a cell. How a virus gets into the body varies. There are four primary methods.

The first way is through the respiratory tract, which is the breathing system. In this method, viruses travel through the air and enter through a person's nose or mouth. The common cold and the flu virus are examples of this type of virus. If someone with a cold sneezes or coughs, for example, the virus enters the air. Another person nearby could then breathe in the virus and become infected.

The second method is through the oral and digestive tract. In this method, viruses travel through food or water. These viruses typically affect the mouth and digestive system, such as the intestines.

The third method is through the genital and anal tracts. Sexual intercourse can spread a virus from one person to the other. Sexually transmitted diseases, or STDs, spread this way. This method is also a primary route for HIV to spread from one person to another.

The final way viruses spread is through breaks in the skin. When the skin is broken, whether it is through a cut, abrasion (such as a scraped knee), or animal or insect bite, a virus has a chance to enter the bloodstream. Rabies is one such disease that spreads through animal bites. Another way that the skin is broken is through needles. Drug users often use needles to inject the drugs into their systems. Health care workers also use needles for a wide variety of purposes, from injecting medicines to taking blood samples for tests. This method is another primary way that HIV spreads.[2]

Some viruses enter the body through more than one method. HIV is one such virus. Viruses can also travel through the body. The primary site is where a virus first enters a person and causes infection. A virus may then travel and infect another part of the body. This is the secondary site.

When a virus first enters a body, it binds to a cell. This is a very specific process, taking place between a virus particle and a protein or molecule on the cell's surface. This protein or molecule is called a receptor. Viruses are able to do this because they have evolved in such a way that they can bind to uninfected cells.[3] Different cells in the body may or may not have the right kind of receptor for a specific virus. This is why some viruses cause one type of disease, while another virus causes a different disease.

After a virus attaches to a cell, it penetrates the cell. The virus then affects the cell in a way that makes it possible for the virus to reproduce, or make copies of itself. These copies can then infect other cells. An infected cell usually releases hundreds of thousands of new virus particles that can then spread to other cells.[4]

How Does HIV/AIDS Affect the Immune System?

HIV affects cells of the body's immune system. The purpose of the immune system is to protect the body from disease. When the immune system fails, the body is at risk of infection from many types of illnesses.

The immune system consists of a very complex group of organs, known as the lymphoid organs. Other organs and body parts that support the immune system include the spleen, thymus, and bone marrow.

The lymphoid organs consist of lymph nodes, which are located throughout the body. The lymph nodes are connected by the lymph vessels, which transport lymph, a clear liquid that carries clear cells called *lymphocytes*. Lymphocytes consist of white blood cells, B cells, and T cells.

White blood cells, created by the bone marrow, are transported throughout the body to fight infection and disease. B cells produce antibodies, which travel through the blood and attach themselves to invaders, such as bacteria, toxins, or foreign

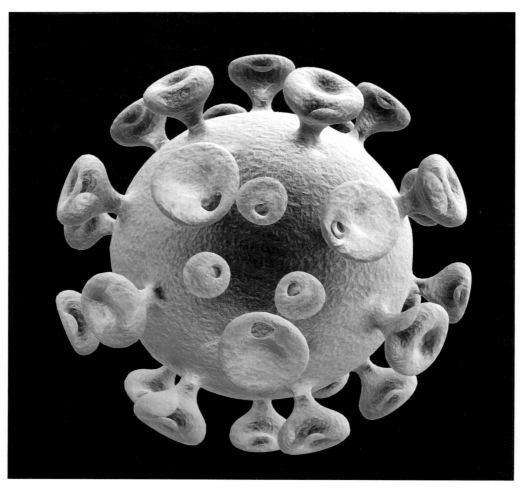

This shows the structure of HIV, the virus that causes AIDS.

blood cells. Antibodies signal the immune system to destroy these unknown particles. T cells attack and destroy unknown diseased cells. They also direct the overall immune response.

T cells include different types of cells. Helper T cells, also known as CD4 cells, tell the B cells to make antibodies. They can also activate other T cells. CD8 T cells attack and destroy infected cells.[5]

HIV attacks and kills T cells, particularly CD4 cells. The

virus then uses CD4 cells to start a process to copy itself. At first, the body is able to produce antibodies that fight HIV, but over time, the body cannot keep up. This means that eventually, HIV overwhelms the body's ability to produce enough antibodies to fight all the HIV particles in the body. The result is that the immune system starts to fail.

When the immune system fails, other infections start to attack the body. These are called *opportunistic infections.* A number of opportunistic infections are common in people with HIV. Full-blown AIDS occurs when these opportunistic infections begin to appear. AIDS is not one specific infection or disease, but a failure of the immune system. Opportunistic infections are what kill people who have AIDS.

One way to track the progress of the disease in the body is by testing the T cell count. In a healthy person, the T cell count ranges from around 600 to 1,200 per cubic millimeter (mm). A person with HIV becomes at risk for contracting the opportunistic

HIV affects the cells of the body's immune system. When the immune system fails, the body is at risk of infection from many types of illnesses.

infections that indicate AIDS (rather than HIV infection) when this number falls below 300 T cells per millimeter.[6] A T cell count below 200 per millimeter is one aspect of an AIDS diagnosis, but it is not the only factor. A person can have a T cell count above 200 per milliliter and still be diagnosed with AIDS.[7]

The Four Stages of HIV Infection

The first stage of HIV infection is the *acute infection stage.* During this time, the virus spreads rapidly through the body, before the body has a chance to recognize it as a foreign invader. Because the virus is reproducing rapidly, during this stage, people are highly infectious to others. There is a high level of the virus present, and people at this stage do not know they are infected. At first, the number of T cells drops before the body is able to respond. Then the immune system goes into full force. The number of T cell increases again, but this is not permanent, and the numbers are not as high as they were before.[8]

People in the very early stages of HIV infection will sometimes have some general symptoms, such as headaches, fatigue, and swollen glands. These symptoms are very common in a number of illnesses, so most people, including physicians, do not suspect HIV infection at this point.

The second stage is the *asymptomatic stage*. This is the longest stage of HIV infection. It lasts about ten years, on average.[9] However, this stage can be as brief as one year or as long as fifteen.[10] Even though the disease is "quiet" during this time, the virus and body are very active. While it seems that nothing is happening inside the body because there are generally no symptoms of illness, the virus continues to replicate and the immune system continues to fight the virus. Darrell E. Ward writes in the 1999 *AmFAR AIDS Handbook* that, during this stage,

> billions of HIV particles are destroyed by the immune system's response to the virus, and an equal number are produced to take their place. Also each day, billions of CD4 lymphocytes are destroyed by HIV, only to be replaced by new cells produced by the immune system.[11]

This daily process takes its toll on the body. During the second stage, the overall CD4 count goes down over time.

Some people begin to develop opportunistic infections, such as mouth sores or minor skin conditions, during the second stage. Many people have no symptoms at all during the second stage. However, medical treatments, called *antiretroviral therapy*, begin at this stage if the person has been diagnosed with

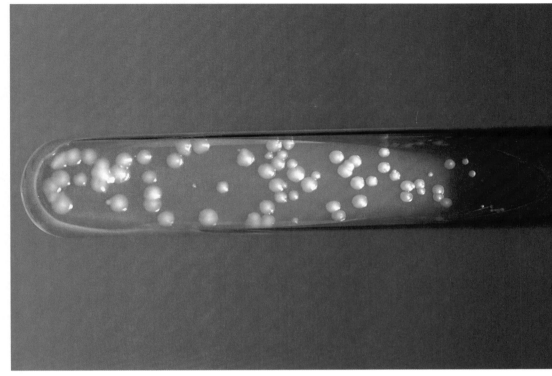

This test tube contains a fungal pathogen, *Cryptococcus neoformans*, which is one type of opportunistic infection developed by people with AIDS.

HIV, which for many people does not occur until symptoms are present. These treatments slow the ability of the virus to multiply.

The third stage is *early HIV disease*. By this time, T cell levels have dropped greatly, and people are at risk for opportunistic infections. Antiretroviral therapy continues at this stage, and treatment for opportunistic infections is added.

The last stage is *advanced HIV disease*, or AIDS. The AIDS diagnosis is made with the presence of opportunistic infections or when the CD4 count is less than 200 cells per milliliter of blood. During this stage, people are at high risk of developing the illnesses that define AIDS. These include a number of bacterial infections, cancers, and viral infections. AIDS-related dementia is also common. This is because AIDS illnesses affect parts of the brain. Muscle loss is another common ailment of AIDS. This is when the body's tissues start to break down.

How Does HIV Spread?

Transmission refers to how the virus spreads. Transmission of HIV occurs in three primary ways.[12]

Sexual Contact. Throughout the world, this is the most common way the virus spreads from one person to another. HIV spreads through both heterosexual and homosexual contact. Sexual transmission is the method by which most HIV infections occur in the United States today. Transmission rates are lower for other means, such as sharing hypodermic needles or through blood transfusions (all blood donated in the United States is tested for HIV infection).

Most sexual transmission occurs through vaginal or anal intercourse. Oral sex can also transmit the virus, although the risk is much lower than with intercourse. Anal intercourse poses the highest level of risk for transmission, because the internal tissue around the anus can tear easily, allowing infected fluids to enter. Male-to-female transmission through vaginal intercourse poses the second-highest risk of transmission. In the developing world where HIV infection is spreading rapidly, vaginal intercourse is the primary method of transmission. Women are a high-risk group.

As many as 90 percent of AIDS cases worldwide result from sexual transmission.[13] Although vaginal intercourse poses the second-highest sexual risk, it is the main method of transmission worldwide.[14] People in the early and late stages of HIV infection have the highest risk of transmitting the disease to someone else—the former because they do not know they are infected.

People who have sexually transmitted diseases or other infections are more likely to become infected when sexually active. This is because these diseases create open sores that make it easier for the bodily fluids of the infected partner to reach the healthy partner. STDs also cause inflammation of the genitals, which means that more white blood cells and T cells are in the genital tissues. Of course, this does not mean that infection can occur only if a person has an STD.

Blood. HIV travels in the bodily fluids and tissues of an infected person, including the blood. As mentioned earlier, one of the ways a virus can spread is through breaks in the skin. The sharing of needles among drug users is the leading cause of blood transmission.[15] If a needle with small bits of infected blood is then injected into a healthy person, the infected blood can come into contact with the healthy blood and transmit the disease. However, simply holding a needle that was previously injected into someone with HIV will not transmit the disease. Contact must be direct.

An early problem in the HIV/AIDS epidemic occurred with blood transfusions. (Blood transfusions involve taking blood from one person and putting it into the body of another.) Infected blood spread the disease rapidly during that time.

In the Western world, HIV tests have been performed on all donated blood since the mid-1980s. This has greatly reduced the risk of transmission through blood products. However, it is still a high-risk factor in other parts of the world.

Health care workers have also been at risk of HIV infection through contact with infected blood. Improved health care practices have lowered the risk to health care workers.

Transmission From Mother to Infant. A pregnant woman can transmit the virus to her baby during birth or through breast-feeding. This is called *perinatal transmission.* Infected women who do not breast-feed and who take HIV drugs prior to giv-ing birth can sometimes avoid transmitting the disease to their babies. This type of transmission in the United States is rare, because HIV-positive women are more likely to give birth by cesarean section and to give their infants formula rather than breast milk. According to the San Francisco AIDS Foundation, the number of mother-to-child transmissions in the United States reached a high of 954 in 1992 and dropped to 48 in 2004, a 95 percent reduction.[16] The rates of transmission are highest among women who do not receive care while pregnant or who are not tested while pregnant.[17] A woman who does not know she is infected obviously carries a greater risk of transmitting the virus to her baby.

How a pregnant woman with HIV is addressed medically depends on many things, such as if she has taken HIV medications during pregnancy, the levels of the virus in her body, and when she started receiving medical care during pregnancy.[18] If an

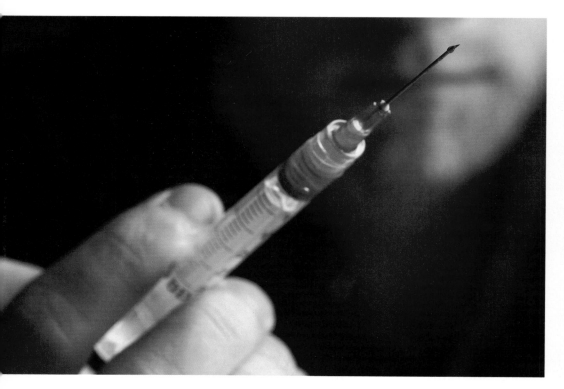

One primary method of HIV transmission is sharing of needles between people who use injected drugs.

infant contracts the disease, the prognosis, or future for that child, is not encouraging. Infants with HIV infection often develop AIDS much faster than older populations.[19]

Although the rate of transmission in the United States could continue to drop (particularly if there is mandatory HIV testing for all pregnant women), this method of transmission is still a concern in other parts of the world. It is the second leading cause of transmission worldwide.[20]

How HIV Does *Not* Spread

While HIV is a global problem, the truth is that the disease does not spread easily in comparison to other viruses. Unlike a cold virus, which travels through the air, direct contact is required for a person to contract HIV.

Casual contact, such as shaking hands, does not spread HIV. Hugging and light kissing does not spread the disease. Open-mouthed kissing, particularly if there are sores inside the mouth, could potentially lead to transmission. HIV has been found in saliva, but the possibility of transmission in this way is highly unlikely. Saliva is considered a "noninfectious" bodily fluid.[21] HIV is not spread through other common forms of contact, such as sharing kitchens or food preparation tools. Nor is it spread by touching walls, doorknobs, or toilet seats. In addition, unlike some viruses, HIV does not spread through insect bites. Other noninfectious bodily fluids include sweat, tears, urine, and feces.[22]

Preventing HIV

Because HIV spreads through very specific ways, prevention is directly related to avoiding and reducing the risks of those methods. This may be easier said than done. Not only is education about the disease required, it also includes changing human behavior. Another significant issue is the availability of prevention methods. In developing countries, all of these factors are problems. In Western countries, where the prevalence of the disease is lower, certain populations are seeing an increase in transmission. For example, the rate of transmission among homosexual males is on the rise after many years of showing a decline.

Sexual transmission is the number one method of spreading the disease. The only way to avoid HIV through sexual contact is to avoid this contact altogether. Abstinence, which is avoiding all sexual contact that might pose a risk, is the only sure way to avoid sexual transmission. This means abstaining from other behaviors besides intercourse; for instance, oral sex poses a risk. For this and other reasons, many people now choose to wait until marriage or until they are in a committed relationship to have sex.

For those who have had sex and are HIV negative, the best choice for remaining HIV free is to abstain from having additional sex or to remain in a monogamous relationship. That means that neither partner has sex with anyone else.

For those who are not in committed relationships, safe sexual practices are required. This can mean many things. Taking part in sexual activities that do not involve direct contact with bodily fluids is one way. This means avoiding oral sex and intercourse.

The chances of HIV transmission can be greatly reduced by the use of condoms. Condoms are made for both males and females. Condoms for males are typically easier to use. Latex or polyurethane condoms are best. Those made from lambskin or other natural materials can allow fluids to pass through. To help prevent infection, condoms need to be used correctly. A new condom must be used each time—for both oral sex and intercourse. Condoms are not 100 percent safe. They can break or slip off during intercourse.

Dental dams are small, square pieces of latex that can be used as a barrier during oral sex on either a male or female. A female condom may also be used as a barrier during oral sex.

Not sharing needles is another way to avoid infection. Drug users are at a high risk of contracting HIV. For one thing, they often share needles, and for another, because drugs interfere with a person's judgment, they often have unprotected sex.

Other prevention programs, such as testing donated blood, decrease the risk of transmission. Health care workers who practice safe handling methods of needles and blood are at a low risk of infection.

One primary concern about the prevention of HIV infection relates to developing countries. Educating large populations takes money and resources. People who do not know how the disease spreads put themselves and others at risk. Some religious practices do not allow the use of condoms. The Roman Catholic Church, for example, does not allow couples to use contraceptives (devices or drugs that prevent pregnancy). Other religious groups oppose the use of condoms because they believe that promoting condom use encourages illicit sexual behavior.

History of the Disease

According to Avert, an organization that, as its name suggests, works to avert HIV and AIDS:

> The origin of AIDS and HIV has puzzled scientists ever since the illness first came to light in the early 1980s. For over twenty years it has been the subject of fierce debate and the cause of countless arguments, with everything from a promiscuous flight attendant to a suspect vaccine [program] being blamed.[1]

Origins of the Disease

No one knows exactly where HIV came from. What is known is that it causes the AIDS disease. Many theories exist as to the origins of the virus. The most commonly accepted theory is that it came from the simian immunodeficiency virus (SIV).[2] SIV is a very similar immunodeficiency virus that affects monkeys. In 1999, researchers from the University of Alabama found a type of SIV that is almost identical to one type of HIV (there are two types of HIV: HIV-1 and HIV-2). The SIV they found came from chimpanzees that were once common in West Africa. Other strains of SIV have been found in African monkeys.[3]

Researchers have known for a long time that some viruses can affect both humans and some animals. The question with HIV is how the virus spread from monkeys to humans. There are many theories about this, but no one has proved how it occurred. Extensive research shows that the virus, or a subtype of the virus, may have killed some people as early as 1959. Three such deaths have been traced to a man in the Democratic Republic of Congo (1959), a teenager in St. Louis, Missouri (1969),[4] and a Norwegian sailor (1976).[5] It is possible that the earliest HIV infections happened in the 1930s.[6]

Researchers continue to try to determine the origins of the disease. Many scientists believe that knowing the history of the virus will help prevent it. Most researchers agree that the first cases of HIV originated in Africa.[7]

In the late 1970s and early 1980s, doctors in the United States started seeing unusual diseases. At that time, most of the patients were homosexual males. On June 5, 1981, Michael Gottlieb published a report in the U.S. Centers for Disease Control's *Morbidity and Mortality Weekly Report (MMWR)*. The report covered five patients who all had a specific and rare type of pneumonia. The article was titled "Pneumocystis Pneumonia, Los Angeles." In the article, Gottlieb reviewed the cases of his patients. All of them were gay men. This report, later recognized as a historic article, did not receive much attention at the time. The *MMWR* ran a second report on July 3, 1981. This article described twenty-six gay men in New York and California who had a rare form of cancer, Kaposi's sarcoma. The media paid more attention this time. Over the next two years, a number of articles appeared in the news. All of the articles described what is now known as AIDS.[8]

Because early cases and reports were among gay men, the disease was first believed to be something that only homosexual men could get. The disease was first known as a gay-related immune disease, or GRID. Researchers quickly learned that this was incorrect. However, it caused a lot of discrimination against homosexuals early in the epidemic.[9] Haitian immigrants (people from Haiti) also showed high levels of AIDS.[10] It did not take long for the disease to reach other populations. According to authors Ronald Bayer and Gerald M. Oppenheimer in *AIDS Doctors: Voices from the Epidemic:*

> Gay men, drug users, blood transfusion recipients, hemophiliacs, the sexual partners of those at risk, and babies born to infected mothers would all be officially diagnosed with AIDS by June 1984, three years after the first case reports. By then, 4,918 cases had been reported to the CDC [U.S. Centers for Disease Control and Prevention]; 2,221 were dead. Less than a year later, in May 1985 . . . the 10,000th case of AIDS [was announced]. It had taken three years for the first 5,000 cases to be reported, 10 months for the second 5,000 cases.[11]

How AIDS Spread Around the World

The advances in technology in the twentieth century had an important impact on the spread of the disease. For the first time in human history, by the mid-1900s, people were able to travel all over the globe easily. This meant that the virus could spread among people who lived very far apart. Medical advances, such as blood transfusions, also contributed to the rapid spread of the disease. Drug use was also on the rise during the 1970s.

In the early stages of HIV infection, transmission occurs primarily through ignorance. People do not know they are

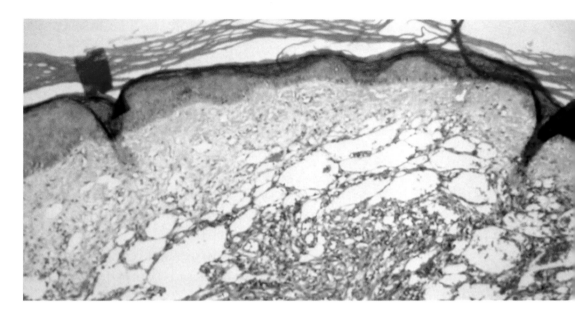

This shows a skin biopsy from a patient with Kaposi's sarcoma, a form of cancer often found in those with AIDS.

infected, and depending on sexual behavior and drug use, the disease can easily spread to a large number of people in a short amount of time.

Ignorance is also a factor in other ways. If people do not know how the disease spreads, then prevention is not possible. People will transmit the disease without knowing it. If it is difficult to educate a large number of people, a disease such as HIV spreads rapidly simply because people are not aware of the problem. This is one of the reasons why AIDS is so difficult to deal with in Africa. In order to educate people, money and resources are needed. Much of Africa is poverty-stricken, so the population does not have access to the information they need. Once people are infected, the same problems make it difficult to treat the disease. The drugs to treat HIV infection can be very expensive. When millions of people are infected, a lot of money is required to get proper treatment for everyone in need.

In a matter of a few years, HIV infection spread across the globe. The disease was first reported in the United States. These cases reported full-blown AIDS. It took a few more years before scientists identified HIV as the cause.

As AIDS spread through the United States, doctors reported cases in Europe as well. Many of the same groups of people were affected as in the United States, such as gay men and drug users. However, cases also developed in immigrants from Central Africa and in those who had traveled to Africa.[12] Before long, cases of HIV infection were reported around the world in all populations, including heterosexuals and children.

By the end of 1986, eighty-five countries had reported cases of AIDS to the World Health Organization (WHO). Of the 38,401 cases reported, most came from the Americas, totaling 31,741, with the second-highest number from Europe, 3,858. Africa followed at 2,323, the Oceania region with 395, and Asia with 84.[13] During the following years, the numbers continued to rise rapidly. Throughout the world, educational programs began, and the United States launched a program in 1988 to educate the public about the disease.[14] In developing countries, where money and educational programs were limited, HIV infection rates continued to rise.

AIDS now affects millions of people worldwide. The World Health Organization described the seriousness of the disease in a September 2002 report. It stated that since the beginning of the known disease, over 20 million people have died. More than 40 million people are infected worldwide. Of those, 95 percent are in the developing world. Of these 95 percent, half of those people are under twenty-four years of age. WHO estimates that if the disease continues the way it has, without serious change, it will affect an additional 45 million people by the year 2010 and will kill another 30 million.[15] According to authors Hung Y. Fan, Ross F. Conner, and Luis P. Villarreal, AIDS "is the fourth-leading cause of death after heart disease, stroke, and acute lower respiratory infections. In Africa, it is the leading cause of death."[16]

At first, how the disease spread was a mystery. Over time, researchers learned how AIDS spreads: through sexual contact, blood, and from mother to infant during or shortly after birth through breast-feeding. However, while the first cases of AIDS were reported in 1981, it was not until 1983 in France, and 1984 in the United States, that researchers isolated HIV as the cause.[17]

Uncovering the virus was significant. First, it answered the question of what caused the breakdown of the immune system. Doctors and researchers now understand how the virus attacks the body. This is important as researchers continue to search for a way to fight the virus. Identifying HIV also led to testing methods. There is no way to test a person for the virus itself. What the tests do is check for antibodies against the virus.

How HIV/AIDS Affects Different Populations

HIV disease eventually affects everyone the same. The result is death from an opportunistic infection. However, up to this point, the disease is very different in the way it affects people around the world. Why? Economic factors and gender play a huge role. In addition, some people are more susceptible than others. This means that some people and conditions make it more likely that a person will contract the virus if exposed. For example, women are more likely to get HIV from an infected male than a male is to get it from an infected female. People who already suffer from an STD are more likely to contract the disease.

Even though the disease first showed up in the gay population, heterosexuals are a high-risk group worldwide. The U.S. Centers for Disease Control and Prevention (CDC) lists certain groups of people worldwide who are more likely to contract

HIV. This is because of their behavior and that of their sexual partners. These groups include:

- People who inject drugs and share injection equipment

- People who abuse other drugs and alcohol (these substances affect a person's judgment)

- People who are paid for sex and their partners

- Children and youth who live on the street

- People in prison

- Men who have sex with other men[18]

In the United States, HIV affects some populations more than others, particularly African Americans and Hispanics. The rates of infection among these two groups is three to six times as high as that in the rest of the population.[19] As is seen in other parts of the world, this may be due to differences in economic conditions.

AIDS also affects other groups in particular ways.

Adolescents. HIV among youth in the United States is an ongoing concern for those who study the disease and its effects. As of early 2004, the CDC reported 40,059 total diagnoses among people aged thirteen to twenty-four in the United States. Since the beginning of the disease, about 10,129 people in this age group died from AIDS.[20] The numbers of young people infected with HIV is growing. The proportion of people aged thirteen to twenty-four with an HIV diagnosis rose from 3.9 percent in 1999 to 4.2 percent in 2004. As is seen in the older population, African-American and Hispanic youths have higher rates of infection. Among those aged thirteen to nineteen, African Americans totaled 66 percent

While the first cases of AIDS in the United States were reported in 1981, it was not until 1983 in France, and 1984 in this country, that researchers isolated HIV as the cause.

Young people are a particular concern for those who study HIV/AIDS. Since the beginning of the disease, more than ten thousand people aged thirteen to twenty-four have died of AIDS.

of reported AIDS cases, and Hispanics made up 21 percent.[21] In the 2000 U.S. census report, the proportion of African Americans in the U.S. population (children and adults) was 12.3 percent, and the proportion of Hispanics was 12.5 percent[22]—which means that a disproportionate number of those with AIDS are African American or Hispanic. The CDC Office of Minority Health lists HIV/AIDS as the seventh-leading cause of death for blacks or African Americans in 2002.[23]

HIV infection in adolescents happens mostly through sexual contact. Almost one quarter of sexually transmitted diseases reported in the United States are among adolescents.[24] This is important because STDs are a high risk factor for contracting

HIV. Additionally, adolescents have a tendency to feel that they are invincible, or that nothing can harm them. The "it won't happen to me" type of thinking may be a contributing factor to unsafe practices. This age group is also less likely to return for medical treatment if they receive a positive diagnosis.[25]

Children. By the end of 2003, 2.5 million children worldwide under the age of fifteen had HIV/AIDS. About half a million children died from AIDS in 2003, with 700,000 new infections in those under fifteen years of age. Sub-Saharan Africa had the highest number of children living with HIV. As of 2003, there were an estimated 3 million children affected in that area.[26] As with the older population, over 95 percent of HIV-infected children live in developing countries.

In the United States, New York City has the highest percentage of children with HIV/AIDS. Miami, Florida, and Washington, D.C., follow. The use of antiretroviral drugs has reduced HIV transmission from pregnant women to their babies.[27] This is not the case in developing countries where access to these drugs is not as available.

Women. Globally, the number of women contracting HIV has been increasing. By the end of 2005, 17.5 million women had HIV. About half of the adults with HIV infection are female. The primary method of contracting HIV for women is heterosexual sex. In the United States, African-American and Hispanic women are at a greater risk. These two groups combined make up less than 25 percent of women in the United States. However, they represent over 79 percent of AIDS cases in women.[28]

Minorities. Minority populations, particularly African Americans and Hispanics, are affected much more in the United States than others. These groups account for more than half of reported AIDS cases. African Americans total about half of the affected people in the United States; however, this group represents only about 12 percent of the total U.S. population. In addition, Hispanics total 15 percent of total AIDS cases and make up only 13 percent of the total U.S. population.[29] Why are these groups affected so unequally? According to a report from the National Institutes of Health (NIH), drug use among these populations is a major problem. Additional activities adding to the spread of the disease among minorities is homosexual sex among males and an increase in transmission through heterosexual sex.[30] Other high-risk behaviors are also seen in these groups as well as in the general population. The NIH reports that by the end of 2003, African-American and Hispanic males totaled 64 percent of all infected males in the United States. Women in these groups represented a total of 83 percent of all women infected in the United States. Additionally, nearly 71 percent of children affected with AIDS fell into these minority groups. For African-American men, AIDS is the leading cause of death for those between the ages of twenty-five and forty-four.[31]

Homosexual and Other Populations. The CDC estimates that about 45 percent of the total U.S. population with HIV are gay and bisexual men. This includes people of all ethnic backgrounds. However, the CDC also warns that this may change because

> heterosexual blacks, women and others infected after having high-risk sex (such as with someone with HIV, an injection-drug user or a man who has sex with other men) now account for a larger proportion of those living with HIV than those who are living with full-blown AIDS.[32]

No longer are gay men and drug users the only ones at high risk.

To summarize, adolescents and women represent the fastest growing populations affected with HIV/AIDS. Women who are infected through heterosexual sex are the fastest growing high-risk population.[33] This in turn puts more children at risk because pregnant women can pass the virus to their babies. For children between the ages of one and four, AIDS is one of the top ten causes of death. Members of minority groups face a much more severe problem than other populations. Adolescents, children, and minority women are in the highest risk groups and represent the most cases of infection of all groups.

Where Is AIDS Most Prevalent Around the World?

Epidemiology is the study of the causes, spread, and control of disease. Epidemiologists conduct complex calculations to estimate current numbers of people infected with various diseases and how fast the problem is expected to grow. The AIDS pandemic—an illness spread across a large geographic area—is being studied by epidemiologists all over the world.

About 40 million people worldwide have HIV/AIDS.[34] Currently, Africa has the worst AIDS problem in the world. However, many other locations have a significant problem as well. If AIDS continues the way it looks as if it will, Asia will soon have a large problem as well. In the Western world, where the disease has been somewhat controlled, certain populations are seeing a rise in AIDS cases. Adolescents and women are among these risk groups.

There is no question that Africa is severely affected by the AIDS pandemic. Other areas are seriously affected as well. Some areas are seeing a rapid growth in the spread of HIV. Unfortunately, HIV is spreading the most in poor areas. AIDS experts Alexander Irwin, Joyce Millen, and Dorothy Fallows write: "Today the disease is advancing in many other regions moving along fault lines of poverty, inequality, and conflict between and within countries."[35] AIDS is a global problem that is not the responsibility of one single country or government. The same authors write: "Current data show that HIV/AIDS is spreading fast in the Caribbean, Asia, and Eastern Europe, as well as in poor urban neighborhoods in the U.S."[36] The global spread of AIDS brings a twofold challenge: reducing rates of transmission and treating those currently affected.

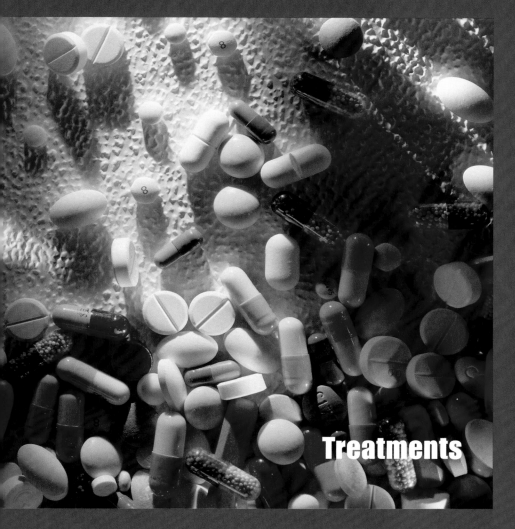

Treatments

At this time, there is no cure for AIDS. Once a person is infected with HIV, the virus will eventually damage the immune system to the point where an opportunistic infection will take the life of the infected person. Currently, the most effective way to treat AIDS (and many other viral infections) is to treat the symptoms and let the virus run its course. Unfortunately, the AIDS virus is fatal. Treating the virus directly is difficult because of how it operates in the body, so the best option is to prevent it. This can be very difficult.

The way viruses attack cells makes them hard to treat. Viruses rely on the cell for replication, so killing the virus means killing the cell. Antibiotics that work on other invaders, such as bacteria and fungi, do not work on viruses. Antibiotics stop the processes of foreign invaders without harming the host. The nature of how viruses operate within the cell, using the cell's energy, makes this method difficult. The closest thing to an antibiotic for a virus is called an *antiviral.* These drugs stop or slow a virus's infection process. Antivirals are important to the future of virus treatments.[1]

HIV belongs to a class of viruses called *retroviruses.* This makes it even more difficult to treat. Retroviruses infect a cell in such a way that the host cell does not die. The infected cell is used to continually make more viruses. In the case of HIV, the body is eventually unable to keep up with the virus's rate of reproduction. This can take many years, however. At first, the body is able to produce antibodies to fight the virus. (HIV tests look for the presence of HIV antibodies.) However, during this time, even if an individual feels fine, the virus may be damaging the immune system. This process may be slowed with medications.[2] This is why testing, even when there are no symptoms, is important to treating the disease. After some time, often a number of years even without treatment, the virus finally takes over and symptoms begin to appear.

Another problem with treating HIV is that the virus mutates, or changes. Mutation is common among all types of viruses. This makes treating HIV difficult. A treatment that works on one type of HIV may not work as well on another type. Additionally, virus mutations can make it difficult to treat people with the current drugs. For example, if the virus mutates, a person may stop responding to a medication that had worked well up to that point. This means changing medications by using different drugs or combinations of drugs. This process can be expensive, and it also means that the infected person needs to have access to different medications. This is not an option for many people in developing countries where access to treatment is limited.

Scientists have developed vaccines for some viruses. Vaccines are made from inactivated or weakened forms of the virus. The body recognizes the vaccine as a foreign presence and makes antibodies. Then, if the live virus enters the body, antibodies are already present to fight the virus. There is no vaccine for HIV. When HIV enters the body, it takes some time before the body recognizes HIV as a foreign entity. By the time the body starts making antibodies, the virus has infected a large number of cells.

The ability of the virus to mutate also causes problems for the development of a vaccine. This means that if scientists developed a vaccine, the virus could change enough so that the vaccine no longer worked against it. Researchers continue to look for ways to attack the virus itself or ways to stop the process in which the virus replicates in cells.

Currently, managing the HIV/AIDS pandemic involves preventing new transmissions and treating those already infected. This includes developing drugs to inhibit HIV, treating opportunistic infections, and, eventually, developing a vaccine. All of these factors are important. Even if a vaccine were available today, treating the millions of people currently infected would still be important. It would also take time and money to make a vaccine available to everyone. HIV would continue to spread until that happened. Therefore, for best results, all forms of HIV prevention and treatment should be pursued.

Current Treatments

Treatment for HIV/AIDS follows a three-part course. First, in the early stages, treatment focuses on healthy living. This can include such things as eating well, getting enough rest, reducing stress, and exercising. Second, treatment also focuses on easing symptoms of infection. This can often be done successfully, as early infections can be minor. Third, as the disease progresses, the use of antiretroviral drugs helps to slow the rate of HIV infection. At this point, frequent medical consultation is best to monitor the effects of the treatment.

Because HIV is resistant to many drugs, proper timing and dosage of drugs is crucial for the best treatment. Also, because opportunistic infections can differ from one person to another, an individualized treatment program is best. However, in some developing countries, general guidelines for large populations can still be effective.

The most effective way to treat HIV infection is by using a combination of medicines. Antiretroviral drugs provide the best results. Highly active antiretroviral therapy (HAART) is currently the preferred treatment. HAART can increase a person's lifespan. HAART medications help fight the various replication cycles of the virus. When combined, these medicines help slow the development of AIDS.

One major issue with HAART treatment is that it is very expensive. By the end of the 1990s, this type of treatment cost more than $20,000 per person each year.[3] Globally, many people who need the treatment most cannot afford it. At this rate, providing drugs to the people in a typical African country "would cost more than the entire national income, leaving nothing over for food and clothes," according to author Emma Guest, who lived in South Africa for a number of years to write about the disease.[4] However, many AIDS organizations are working to lower the cost of drugs and are making progress.

Developing New Drugs and Potential Vaccines

Researchers across the globe are working to develop new drugs to treat and, it is hoped, eventually prevent HIV. These include both antiretrovirals and potential vaccines. This is a lengthy process: Currently, developing and testing a drug successfully can take up to ten years.[5] In the United States, before a drug is available on a broad scale, it must have Food and Drug Administration (FDA) approval. This requires a multistep process of conducting clinical trials. These are complicated and take time. However, the purpose of these trials is to ensure that the drugs are effective and safe. If this part of the process is skipped, unsafe medicines could enter the market. The testing process allows researchers to determine if the drugs are effective. Sometimes a drug may work wonderfully in a laboratory but not work so well in human trials. If a drug were to be approved based only on laboratory studies, it could have negative results. The drug may not work as well as expected, could be danger-ous, and could create false hope.[6]

While a vaccine would be ideal, researchers question whether it is even possible. There are many different strains of HIV, and a different vaccine may be required for each. Addi-tionally, because HIV mutates, a fully efficient vaccine may not be possible. As a result, some researchers believe a vaccine that suppresses HIV infection is more realistic. This type of vaccine, called a therapeutic vaccine, would boost the immune sys-tem's ability to fight HIV.[7] (While a traditional vaccine prevents a disease, a therapeutic vaccine helps the body fight a virus.) One French study of a therapeutic vaccine showed a decrease of HIV virus in the body by an average of 80 per-

> Highly active antiretroviral therapy, or HAART, is currently the preferred treatment for HIV infection. HAART can increase a person's lifespan by slowing the development of AIDS.

cent after four months. However, no vaccine, whether therapeutic or preventive, is likely to be approved for years.[8]

In studying vaccine opportunities, scientists look at the two different ways the vaccine activates the immune system. One way is by activating the body's killer cells, which seek out and kill viruses. The other way is by creating antibodies against the virus.

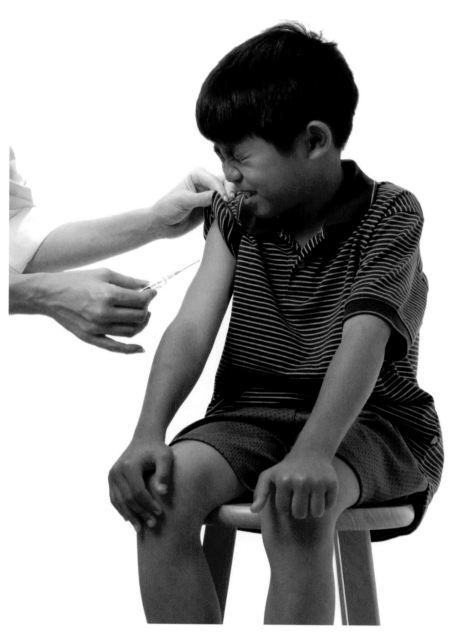

Researchers are looking for a vaccine that would either prevent HIV or suppress the infection. But it is likely to be many years before either type of vaccine is available.

One of the biggest problems in developing a vaccine is that researchers often test vaccines in animals. There are no animals that react to HIV in exactly the same way that humans do. The closest animals are monkeys, who have reactions to SIV that are similar to human reactions to HIV. However, monkeys are expensive. In addition, many animal-rights activists oppose the use of them for research.[9] This further prolongs the process. Before conducting human clinical trials, the safety of the drugs needs to be determined.

In developing new drugs and vaccines, researchers consider how and when the drugs will be taken. For example, current HAART treatment involves taking a large number of drugs. When and how much a person takes these medications is part of treatment, because the drugs are most effective when taken at the prescribed times and in the correct amount. Basically, HAART treatment is complicated. One goal in developing new drugs is making the process simpler.

Research and development of both antiretroviral drugs and vaccines are essential for HIV/AIDS treatment. With the huge numbers of people infected, antiretroviral therapies are necessary to slow the progression of the disease. Further, though experts have hope that a preventive vaccine can be developed, it is still a long way off. A full vaccine may never be possible, and so a therapeutic vaccine in combination with other drug therapies may be the best solution.

In 2003, a potential vaccination called AIDSVax, developed by VaxGen, Inc., made it to phase three testing, the first AIDS vaccine to do so. VaxGen hoped that the drug would prevent 30 percent of infections. This is a much lower level of prevention than most vaccines provide, but it is better than no vaccine at all. However, the trial showed that the drug did not work as hoped. Though the trial was unsuccessful, it was still useful for researchers deciding where to focus ongoing studies.[10]

Costs of Treatment

It can take years for a new drug to be made and approved. The drug must go through a long testing process to make sure that new drugs are safe. Otherwise, they could cause more harm than good.

The average cost to use the recommended combination of drug therapies can be as much as $15,000 annually. The cost of generic drugs is less. Generic drugs are those that are chemically identical to brand-name drugs but are produced by another company. When a pharmaceutical company makes a drug, the combination of ingredients is protected by law. For a certain amount of time, no other companies can make that drug. Once the time limit has passed, other companies can make drugs using the same ingredients. However, because the need for affordable HIV drugs is so pressing, there has been a lot of controversy over this process. In 2000, for example, the U.S. government supported its drug manufacturers in a legal disagreement with some countries that used less expensive imitation drugs for AIDS. After negative publicity, the drug companies backed down and dropped the suit. However, policies about drug rights continued to be a problem, with some drug companies still asking for payments from generic drug companies. Basically, people died because they could not afford the medicines.[11]

Generic drugs are now available for many HIV drugs. These are just as effective as the originals. With the availability of generic drugs, the annual cost is now as low as $300 in some African nations. One estimate puts the cost as low as $148 per year.[12] However, when multiplied by the millions of people who need the drugs, this can still be a very large number. Many poor and developing countries cannot afford the medications for the number of people who need them. Additionally, ongoing treatment is required, not just one year's worth. However, the drop in cost for generic medications is significant. The use of generic drugs makes treatment much more possible for the millions of people infected.

HAART consists of five drugs that, taken together, are typically used to treat people with HIV. These are D4T (stavudine), 3TC (lamivudine), NVP (nevirapine), AZT (zidovudine), and EFZ (efavirenz). The World Health Organization recommends combining three of these drugs (such as AZT, 3TC, and NVP) as a first step for treating large numbers of people where individualized treatment programs are difficult.[13] Huge numbers of these drugs are required to treat everyone who needs them. This means high manufacturing costs, distribution costs, and costs associated with teaching people how to take the medications. Even with these large numbers, however, the cost of actually manufacturing drugs is much less than the costs for developing new ones.

Costs increase when the need for health care workers is added. Qualified doctors and nurses are needed to treat patients, provide accurate information about the disease, and explain how to use medications correctly. When HIV-positive patients develop AIDS, the cost of hospitalization, if available, is also very high. Many people in poor countries, where the most people are infected, do not have these options.

The United Nations reports that the annual cost of treating someone with HIV infection dropped 90 percent between 2000 and 2003. Despite this, by December 2004, of the 6 million people who needed treatment, only 700,000 had access to it.[14]

5   AIDS in the United States

The AIDS epidemic may not be as severe in the United States
as it is in other parts of the world. However, this does not mean
that it is under control or not a worry in the United States. In
fact, the spread of HIV/AIDS is increasing in some populations, including the original group most at risk—gay men.
While this group showed a decrease in the proportion of HIV
cases in the 1990s, new infections among this group have
increased since 2001.[1] Adolescents are also a high-risk group. So
are women and members of minority groups, particularly
African Americans and Hispanics.

The CDC estimated that between 1,039,000 and 1,185,000

people in this country had HIV/AIDS by the end of 2003. (It can take over a year to compile information and create statistics.) The wide range between these figures results from a number of factors. Not all states report figures the same way. Anonymous home tests are not included in the reported figures. And one in four people with HIV have not had their infection diagnosed, which means they are not reported.[2]

The CDC calculates these numbers based on reports from each state. All states report positive HIV testing results. HIV test reports are required to keep track of HIV infection for public health reasons. Epidemiologists use this information to observe if a disease is spreading, where, and by how much. This information tells researchers if the epidemic is getting better, staying the same, or getting worse. It also helps the government and other public health agencies determine the best options for public education and prevention methods. For example, the number of pediatric cases (those among infants and young children) has declined because of public health services and education. Voluntary HIV testing by pregnant women and the use of medications has reduced the number of these cases.[3]

Testing, Reporting, and Human Rights

In order to track HIV/AIDS for epidemiological purposes, all states must report any AIDS diagnoses to the health department of that state. This information is used to generate statistics such as the ones used in this book and others. In 1999, the CDC recommended that all states report positive HIV tests. Most states are currently doing so. This is to create better records of tracking the disease from the time of identification to full-blown AIDS.[4] Reports for the United States used by the CDC come from the fifty states, the District of Columbia, and five additional areas associated with the United States (American Samoa, Guam, the Northern Mariana Islands, Puerto Rico, and the U.S. Virgin Islands).[5]

There are three types of testing methods used by the states: anonymous, confidential, or anonymous and confidential. Anonymous testing means that no name is associated with the test. Confidential testing is where the person's name is recorded with the test, but the name is not released publicly. Only those who work with the information see the names, and these people must keep the information private. States must report the results of HIV tests to the CDC for compiling statistics. With name-based reporting, a person's name is reported to the state with a positive HIV test. No other information is provided. As of June 2006, forty-nine states and areas used name-based reporting and six states used code-based reporting.[6] In code-based reporting, names are not used; instead, codes are used to indicate the test results. In name-to-code-based reporting, a person's name is used first and is later replaced with a code. One state, Montana, uses name-to-code-based reporting.[7]

Some people oppose name-based reporting. They argue that it violates patient confidentiality and that it will keep people from being tested. People may fear discrimination or other negative outcomes from being listed by name on reports. These people may choose not to be tested. If they are positive for the virus, they can then spread the disease without knowing it. Those against name-based reporting say this scenario can be avoided through the use of codes or other systems that do not use names.[8] In addition, if someone's name is associated with the disease, he or she may be discriminated against. What if names are accidentally released? This happened in 2005 in Florida, when the names of HIV-positive persons were emailed to eight hundred public health employees.[9]

People who support name-based HIV testing argue that it is the most effective method for tracking new HIV cases. Names are also used when tracking the progression of the disease. It also makes it easier to notify an infected person's partners.[10] How so? If, for example, people received notices saying that someone they had been with tested positive for HIV, they may not take it as seriously as if the notices gave the infected person's name. The CDC recommends that anyone who tests positive for HIV receive counseling, which includes partner notification help. Some health care providers will offer to help a person list and track down previous partners. This is easier when done by name.[11]

Home tests are also an option that is currently available, but the person must send a sample of his or her blood to a laboratory for testing. A professional counselor provides the test results over the phone. Home tests that do not need to be sent

A technician reads an HIV test and notes the results. Testing and reporting are handled in a number of ways in different states.

to a laboratory are also in development. One such test was submitted for FDA approval in October 2005. If approved, the test will contain information on the disease and include a phone number people can call for additional support.[12]

Which Populations Are Most Affected?

Overall, the number of AIDS diagnoses is increasing. Between 2000 and 2004, the United States saw an 8 percent increase in the number of new cases. During this same time, the death rate from AIDS decreased, with a significant decrease from 2003 to 2004. This is because of better medical treatments.[13] In 2003, 17,849 deaths were reported, compared to 15,798 in 2004.[14] However, AIDS is still fatal, and there is no cure. In 2004, nearly 39,000 new diagnoses occurred, and nearly 16,000 people died from HIV/AIDS. The CDC estimated that over 415,000 people in the United States were living with HIV/AIDS in 2004. In addition, because of better medical care, more people are now living with HIV/AIDS. The figure increased 30 percent from 2000 to 2004.[15] Overall, over 529,000 estimated deaths occurred due to AIDS from the first known cases in the United States to the end of 2004. This included 523,598 adults and adolescents and 5,515 children under the age of thirteen.[16]

Based on information from all fifty states, the CDC estimates that about forty thousand people in the United States will become infected with HIV each year. The people with the most infections continue to be men who have sex with men. Heterosexual contact is the second-leading method of transmission. The majority of those infected—three quarters—are male. This includes both adolescent and adult males.[17]

This does not mean that females are "safe." A woman is more likely to pick up the virus through heterosexual sex than a man is. In other words, a female is more likely to get HIV from a male than a male is from a female.

In 2004, most of the infected males—65 percent—were men who had sex with men. The second-highest proportion of males infected, 16 percent, were infected through heterosexual contact. Fourteen percent were injection-drug users, and 5 percent both had sex with men and used injection drugs, so that the exact cause of transmission is unknown.[18]

Women living with HIV/AIDS in the United States totaled an estimated 123,405 in 2004. Of these, 71 percent became infected through heterosexual contact, and 27 percent through injection-drug use. The remaining 2 percent contracted the disease in other ways, including blood transfusion and perinatal transmission.[19]

Even though more men are infected than women, the *rate* at which women are contracting the disease is higher. In 1992, women made up 14 percent of adults and adolescents living with AIDS. This increased to 23 percent by the end of 2004. From 2001 to 2004, the estimated number of AIDS cases increased one percent among males, but 15 percent among females.[20] (These figures do not represent all the women living with HIV infection, only those living with AIDS.) These figures are based on estimates from thirty-five areas (thirty-three states, Guam, and the Virgin Islands) that have long-term, confidential reporting. This allows for tracking from HIV infection to AIDS development.

As mentioned, African Americans and Hispanics are disproportionately infected. African Americans accounted for half of HIV/AIDS diagnoses in 2004.[21] Whites follow, with 30 percent of total infections. Hispanics represent 18 percent.[22]

Not surprisingly, states with the highest number of people also have the highest number of total reported HIV/AIDS cases. New York and California are among the top. North Dakota has the fewest. All fifty states have reported cases.[23]

What do all these numbers mean? In terms of education and prevention, these numbers indicate the groups that require the

Speaking Out

A July 2003 article in a New Orleans weekly newspaper raised awareness about the rising numbers of African-American women contracting HIV in that city. One third of new HIV cases in New Orleans in 2002 were among women, and most of those were African American. For those women quoted in the article, speaking out came with risks: Their family members could be afraid of being infected, their children could be teased, or their friends could abandon them.

Promise, one of the women, contracted the virus soon after her sixteenth birthday as the result of a sexual assault. After her diagnosis, she made a point of educating others about the disease. She had a red ribbon tattooed on the back of her neck, a symbol of AIDS awareness. When others asked her about it, she used the opportunity to educate people about HIV. In Missouri, where she lived at the time of her diagnosis, she started speaking to students in high schools to raise awareness. Later, she moved to New Orleans to continue her work as an advocate. Promise said, "The more people are going to shelter themselves and isolate . . . the more HIV is going to spread. That's what our next generation of kids will face."[24]

most attention. For example, continued outreach to men who have sex with men is necessary, as this group still has the highest rate of infection. However, this group is not growing the fastest as far as new infections are concerned. New female infections are a fast-growing group. Most of these infections come from heterosexual sex. This means that females need to know how to protect themselves. After abstinence, using condoms is the best way to prevent transmission. Minority groups also represent a large group of infections. Women who are members of minority groups are at the greatest risk. Again, education and prevention is needed for people in these groups. For all people infected with HIV/AIDS, treatment options are required. However, many people, particularly in minority groups, cannot afford treatment. This issue needs to be addressed.

What Is the United States Doing to Prevent and Treat HIV/AIDS?

The CDC is the primary government agency working on AIDS education and prevention in the United States. (Additional agencies are involved in the global AIDS problem.) The CDC is part of the U.S. Department of Health and Human Services. It was founded in 1946 to help control malaria. It continues to work toward controlling and preventing infectious and chronic diseases as well as preventing injuries, reducing workplace hazards, addressing disabilities, and helping control environmental health threats.[25]

Regarding HIV/AIDS, the CDC collects information, makes that information available to the public, provides educational materials, and awards grants, among other activities. It offers very thorough information on the HIV/AIDS epidemic throughout the United States and the world.

One of the better-known programs the CDC sponsors for fighting AIDS in the United States is called "Advancing HIV Prevention." The program has four strategies:

1. Incorporate HIV testing as a routine part of care in traditional medical settings.
2. Implement new models for diagnosing HIV infections outside medical settings.
3. Prevent new infections by working with people diagnosed with HIV and their partners.
4. Further decrease mother-to-child HIV transmission.[26]

One of the program's primary goals is to shorten the time between HIV infection and testing. This helps prevent further transmission and allows those infected to obtain medical help earlier. Another aspect of the program is to fund various state plans to combat HIV/AIDS. The CDC's Division of Adolescent and School Health (DASH) is geared toward educating young people in the United States and promoting their health.

A woman receives AIDS information in the mail in the 1980s as part of a public awareness campaign. Education is an important part of AIDS prevention efforts.

DASH provides a variety of information on HIV/AIDS and prevention. Other CDC divisions involved in HIV/AIDS include the Division of HIV/AIDS Prevention, the Division of Sexually Transmitted Diseases, and the National Prevention Information Network. Additional government agencies involved in combating AIDS include the National Institutes of Health (NIH), the Health Care Financing Administration, and the Substance Abuse and Mental Health Services Administration.

The Office of National AIDS policy oversees HIV/AIDS information in the United States. President Bush asked for $22.8 billion in funds to support U.S. and global HIV/AIDS activities in 2007. This request included an additional $1.7 billion above the 2006 funds. Congress was set to vote on approving the funds toward the end of 2006. The domestic funds would support HIV/AIDS medical care (supported through Medicaid and Medicare); cash and housing assistance; prevention, including increased testing; and research.

Global funds would support the President's Emergency Plan for AIDS Relief, or PEPFAR, a five-year program to support AIDS efforts worldwide. Some of these funds would also support the Global Fund to Fight AIDS, Tuberculosis, and Malaria.[27]

The Ryan White CARE Act is another important aspect of the government's HIV/AIDS program. It was first enacted in 1990 and was renewed in 2000. As of 2006, changes from the previous year were still under review. The act's purpose is to improve the quality and availability of care for people with HIV/AIDS who could not otherwise obtain treatment. It is run by the HIV/AIDS Bureau of the Health Resources and Services Administration. It provides funding to both public and private organizations in the states and U.S. territories. The funds help those groups create and run programs. This way, the most people affected with HIV and their families will be helped.[28]

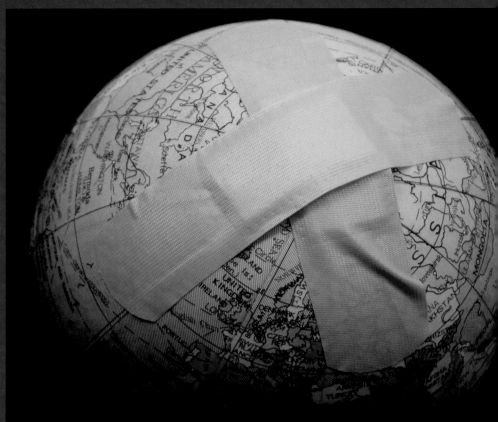

AIDS Around the World

HIV/AIDS is widespread throughout the world. While it affects some countries more than others, everyone is affected by the pandemic. One primary concern about HIV/AIDS around the world is that it tends to hit people in the prime of their lives. Never before has a disease affected this age group so much. People between the ages of twenty-four and forty-five typically represent a huge part of the workforce in any country. As people in this group fall ill and die, they leave jobs unattended and millions of children and elderly people on their own.

Because the epidemic is growing rapidly in Africa and Asia, most of the global discussion focuses on these areas. This is not to minimize problems with HIV/AIDS in other parts of the world. However, as epidemiologists study these areas and determine the best way to combat the problem, lessons learned can be applied to other areas. If programs are successful in Africa, for example, then they can be used elsewhere to slow the spread of the disease and treat those already infected. Most experts agree that a combination of efforts is required to address the global AIDS issue effectively.[1] Those infected must be treated with medications and prevention programs must be in place. Further, ongoing research into better medicines and potential vaccines are needed.

Latin America

In this region, most cases of HIV/AIDS are in urban areas. Brazil has one of the highest rates of infection. As in the United States, in the beginning most cases were among gay men, followed by injection-drug users. HIV/AIDS is now spreading through heterosexual contact with increasing frequency in Mexico, Central America, and South America.[2]

Western Europe

In some respects, the HIV/AIDS epidemic in Western Europe is similar to that in the United States. Treatment is more available, more affordable, and fewer people are dying each year from the virus. However, thousands of new HIV cases occur each year, and a large number of people do not know they are infected.[3] Another concern in Western Europe is the resistance of the virus to some antiretroviral drugs.[4] That is, in some cases, it is not responding to the drugs as well as it used to.

Recent information shows that most of the new HIV infections are transmitted through heterosexual contact. This method of transmission increased 122 percent between 1997 and 2002.[5] Unlike the United States (and Canada), however, many new infections are among migrant people who came to

Europe from high-risk countries. These include sub-Saharan Africa and the Caribbean.[6] The cases among men who have sex with men are also increasing, but not as much as in previous years. HIV/AIDS is the fastest-growing health concern in the United Kingdom.[7] By the end of 2004, an estimated 58,300 adults in Britain were living with HIV. Of these, it was estimated that a third were unaware of their infection.[8] In Germany, overall infection is fairly low.

> One primary concern about HIV/AIDS around the world is that it tends to hit people between the ages of twenty-four and forty-five. As people in this group die, they leave jobs unattended and millions of children and elderly people on their own.

In France, 81 percent of those with HIV are male and 19 percent are female. France began mandatory HIV reporting only in 2003. As a result, it is difficult for experts to analyze the situation there. As in Western Europe in general, the fastest growing method of transmission is through heterosexual sex. The number of cases involving gay men and injection-drug users have decreased.[9]

Spain has the highest number of cumulative cases in Europe—that is, from the beginning of the epidemic, Spain has had the highest total number of reported cases of any European country. Unlike the rest of Europe, most of the reported cases in Spain are among injection-drug users (63 percent). With the availability of HAART, the number of deaths in Spain has declined significantly.[10]

Eastern Europe and Central Asia

The HIV/AIDS epidemic is far worse in Eastern Europe than in Western Europe. Until the mid-1990s, this region had a low infection rate. However, since that time, the epidemic has worsened, and it shows no signs of slowing.[11]

The Russian Federation, Ukraine, and Baltic states are the

The Moscow subway. In Russia, new AIDS cases doubled between 1998 and 2002.

worst affected. In Russia, new cases of HIV doubled from 1998 to 2002.[12] Between 2000 and 2004, 75 percent of the infections reported in Eastern Europe were among people under age thirty.[13] Some estimates predict that without a prevention plan, by the year 2010, between 5 and 8 million Russians may be infected.[14] High-risk behavior among young people, especially the use of injected drugs, is the largest contributor to the problem. Infection through drug use accounted for more than 80 percent of infections in the Russian Federation since the beginning of the epidemic there.[15] Young men have the highest numbers of infections, although infections in women are on the rise. Of particular concern is the high rate of mother-to-child transmission.[16]

More than a million people in Eastern Europe and Central Asia—which includes Kazakhstan, the Kyrgyz Republic, Tajikistan, and Uzbekistan—now have HIV/AIDS. A 2005 report by the World Bank, an organization that gives support to developing countries, states that Europe and central Asia still may be able to prevent the massive population changes that can result from large numbers of AIDS deaths. With proper support, these areas can avoid the devastating population changes that have occurred in southern Africa and other developing regions. This would mean fewer orphans and healthier working-age people. Without support, however, the report states that "AIDS could have a major impact on economic growth, on families, and on future generations."[17] This is particularly important because such a large percentage of people infected are young. With so many people in Eastern Europe under the age of thirty, the disease will hit as this group reaches the age where most people are in the middle of their working lives and raising families. This could create an economic and family crisis very similar to the one now happening in Africa.

Asia and the Pacific

Asia and the Pacific regions are second only to Africa in the number of people currently living with HIV/AIDS.[18] By the end of 2005, an estimated 8.3 million people were living with HIV in Asia, and over two thirds of those were living in India.[19] China has one of the world's largest populations. By 2002, an estimated one million people there had the disease. Some figures project that China may see as many as 15 million people infected by 2010. India is another high-risk nation. It is estimated that total infections could reach as high as 25 million there by 2010.[20] India's epidemic covers a wide geographic range. In some areas, the highest rates of transmission are among drug users, while in other areas, most of those infected contracted HIV through heterosexual sex. Overall, 80 percent

An estimated one million people in China were infected with HIV as of 2002. Many of them live in rural areas, which makes treatment difficult.

of HIV infections in India are transmitted through heterosexual sex.[21] As with Eastern Europe, many infections are in people under the age of thirty. Groups with the highest risk include people who work in the sex industry, those who travel for work (migrant workers), injection-drug users, and truck drivers.[22]

In India, providing education and prevention is difficult. Many infected people are shunned, even by health care workers. India also has many different languages and dialects, which makes creating educational materials a challenge. Some people wrongly believe that the epidemic is limited to high-risk groups only. Some who are infected keep this information secret out of fear of discrimination.[23]

Some of the more difficult issues in addressing the growing

AIDS problem in China are that many of those infected live in rural areas. This makes both prevention education and treatment difficult. Many rural areas do not have the skilled medical staff found in urban areas. Many transmissions in China occur through drug use. Estimates from 2005 indicated that drug users totaled 44 percent of those with HIV infection in China. People who had donated blood or plasma in the past constituted just over 24 percent. Those infected through heterosexual transmission made up 20 percent, while men who have sex with men totaled just over 11 percent. Together, mother-to-child transmission and infected blood products caused one percent of infections.[24]

Due to the large population, China has a high number of people, primarily females, who work in sex industries. These activities are illegal in China, but prevalent. An additional problem is that people who work in sex industries also engage in other high-risk behavior, such as using injection drugs.[25] This group is at high risk of contracting the virus and transmitting it to the men with whom they have sex. The men then transmit the virus to their wives, and their wives to their babies.

The situation in Africa, particularly sub-Saharan Africa (roughly the southern two thirds of the continent), is serious. Currently, Africa has the most HIV/AIDS infections in the world. About 70 percent of those infected worldwide live in sub-Saharan Africa.[1] More than 24 million people are infected, and approximately 2.7 million new infections occurred in 2005. Two million people died from the virus between 2004 and 2005.[2] The epidemic has seriously affected young people in this region. Nearly 2 million youths under age fifteen are infected, and over 12 million children are orphans because of the epidemic.[3]

In addition to the large numbers of people currently affected, the number of people who will be directly impacted will continue to rise. This is because many people becoming infected now and in the near future will not become ill with AIDS for a number of years.[4]

The epidemic influences countries differently. Some are more affected than others are, and some have plans that create better results (the efforts in Uganda are one example). Overall, however, the average life expectancies throughout the region have dropped from around seventy years of age to the thirties and forties.

Who Is Most Affected?

For the most part, Africa is made up of what Westerners refer to as "developing countries." That is, the countries have a low average income, less structured governments, and lower levels of literacy, education, child welfare, and life expectancy compared with other countries around the globe. The AIDS crisis puts these countries even further behind the rest of the world. The dramatic decrease in life expectancies caused by AIDS, for example, reverses the progress made in this area. The huge orphan crisis only makes the problem of child welfare (the well-being of children) even worse that it would be without the added problem of a serious health epidemic.

About 70 percent of those with HIV/AIDS worldwide live in sub-Saharan Africa. More than 24 million people are infected, and approximately 2.7 million new infections occurred in 2005.

Because the millions of people affected by HIV/AIDS are generally poor, a number of problems arise. The governments of these countries cannot afford the type of education and prevention programs necessary to slow the rate of transmission.

Further, money is not available to treat those already infected. For those who have AIDS now, the health care system is not adequate. For those infected but not yet ill, the medications needed to slow the progression of the disease are not affordable.

In general, the health care in these countries is not as established as in Western countries. This means that those infected are more likely to fall ill sooner. The basic health care that can help someone in the United States remain healthy for a long time before AIDS is simply not available for millions of people. Malnutrition is a serious problem. AIDS activist and writer Emma Guest writes: "They can't afford enough food, clean drinking water and the drugs to treat opportunistic infections, let alone the cocktails of antiretroviral drugs that keep HIV-positive North Americans and Europeans alive for years."[5] What many Westerners take for granted, such as clean drinking water, is not available for millions of Africans.

The people dying from AIDS are the ones who would normally contribute to the economy and raise families. The food crisis in Africa is affected by AIDS because those who grow food are dying. AIDS expert Susan Hunter writes: "Recent food emergencies in that region have put 14.4 million people at risk of starvation, in part because 7 million agricultural workers have died from AIDS since 1985."[6]

As elsewhere, women have higher rates of infection in sub-Saharan Africa than do men. For every two men infected, three women are infected. Females are also infected at earlier ages. Among those aged fifteen to twenty-four, an average of three women are infected for every man.[7]

Susan Hunter says, "HIV infection in teens will continue to define the epidemic and global population structure for the next three decades."[8] Globally, over half of those infected with HIV are under the age of twenty-five. This group then becomes ill during the prime family and working years. In addition, because this group is younger and healthier, they live longer and

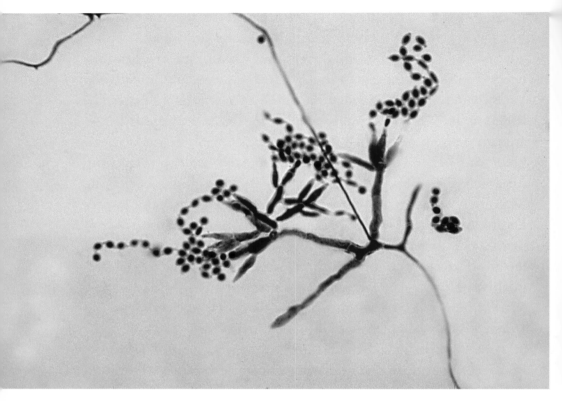

This microorganism causes penicilliosis, one of the opportunistic infections that can affect people with AIDS. In Africa, treatment for such infections is often hard to obtain.

require more treatment, which adds to the already stretched resources.

Addressing the Problem

The problem in this region (and all across the globe) involves more than simply preventing new infections. A plan that attacks many aspects of the problem is needed. Preventive measures must be established. Treatment for those currently infected needs to be ensured. Finally, the huge numbers of orphaned children need some type of assistance. Despite the number of deaths caused by AIDS, births continue to outnumber deaths.

In many parts of Africa, having a large family is desirable. In 2000, the average woman in Uganda had a family of seven children. In other areas, the average woman had five or six children.[9] This means that as parents die from AIDS, large numbers of children are orphaned. Someone needs to provide help and guidance for these millions of children.

Many challenges face the region in addressing all the areas that need attention. One significant barrier to meeting these challenges is money. The funding required to introduce educational programs, pay for medicines and related health care, and treat those infected with AIDS is very high. Even if governments were to supply only basic preventive methods, such as condoms, the total cost would be hundreds of millions of dollars to provide them to all of Africa.[10] Even if this were possible, people would then have to know why condoms are important and how to use them. While this may seem simple, high rates of illiteracy combined with limited media exposure and religious objections make this difficult.

Education about the disease is problematic in other ways as well, not just in preventive methods, such as using condoms. In order to prevent transmission effectively, people need to know more than simply how and why to use a condom. People first need to know what the virus is, how it spreads, and how it can be prevented. Then people need to change behaviors, which is not an easy task. For example, it is highly unlikely that people will stop having sex. Instead, informing people of alternative practices, such as using condoms and limiting sexual partners, is necessary. Further, this only works if large groups of people accept the ideas. Some religions, for example, do not want to promote the use of condoms. This can have detrimental results. In 1998, the former president of Zambia declared advertising condoms illegal. This happened right after the Catholic Church threatened to withdraw its support of his presidential election campaign.[11]

Nationwide support is also necessary. For three years, South African President Thabo Mbeki blocked a national program protecting infants because he did not believe that HIV causes AIDS.[12] This shows how problems can occur in unexpected ways. (Mbeki eventually changed his viewpoint.)

Hope in Uganda

While it may seem impossible to make the changes needed to battle AIDS, this is not necessarily the case. It is true that a great deal more funding and effort are required, but change can occur. Various programs are showing promise. Uganda, for example, has been very successful in stabilizing its AIDS crisis. While there are still many people infected, the country has been able to keep the crisis under control. The Global AIDS Program (GAP) is part of the CDC; it helps countries worldwide to address the AIDS problem. According to a report published by GAP, Uganda's efforts in fighting AIDS have been comprehensive and effective.

The rates of HIV in Uganda have been cut in half since 1992. Still, the overall rate of HIV is 7 percent of the total population (the global goal is to keep it under one percent). As in other parts of the world, the primary method of transmission is through heterosexual sex. Nearly a quarter of new transmissions are from mother to child. However, despite these high numbers, Uganda's program is a model for the rest of sub-Saharan Africa.[13]

Uganda was one of the first countries to see the need for some type of program, beginning in 1986.[14] Uganda's program, which is coordinated through the Uganda AIDS Commission, has many important features. These include strong public commitment, education, political openness about HIV/AIDS, realization of the true threat of AIDS to all of society, and cooperation among many organizations.

While Uganda still has a big problem to deal with, its

Because of AIDS, millions of African children have been orphaned. Even those with healthy families are affected, since so many teachers and other adults have died.

success in public outreach and drastically reducing the number of HIV/AIDS cases shows that it can be done. As with any program, one main component is money. Uganda's program works with a variety of partners. One of the main reasons why the program in Uganda is successful is because it involves many areas. The program does not focus only on prevention, for example. Nor does it rely on only one agency. The program incorporates education, public support, and many different service organizations.

People in Uganda, from political figures to service workers, are willing to talk openly about the disease. Martha Ainsworth, an AIDS expert with the World Bank, expressed the opinion that one reason governments do not want to take responsibility for the AIDS problem is because it means talking openly about sex.[15] Until people are willing to discuss modes of transmission, educational efforts will not be successful. The political figures in Uganda are willing to talk about HIV/AIDS, and this has made a difference. Open talk is only one part of the issue, however. Funding needs—ranging from money for educational programs to money for drugs—continue to be a major issue.

Unfortunately, there has been an increase in infection recently in Uganda. Some believe this is in part because of the U.S. government's insistence on promoting abstinence over condoms in countries where the United States provides funding for AIDS prevention.[16]

Pharmaceuticals

When countries in Africa filed a lawsuit against pharmaceutical companies for the right to produce patented drugs at a lower cost, they made progress. However, the World Trade Organization and the United States supported the pharmaceutical companies' rights to protect their drug formula, or "recipe," against other companies that want to produce cheaper versions. Because so many people need these drugs, there is a lot of money involved.

Nkosi's Haven

In July 2000, a young boy delivered a speech about AIDS that he wrote himself. He gave the speech at the 13th International Aids Conference in Durban, South Africa. Because the speech was televised worldwide, he reached millions of people.

Nkosi Johnson was born with HIV, and at age eleven he was the oldest child born with HIV to survive in South Africa. His mother was unable to care for him because of her own illness. Gail Johnson adopted Nkosi, and together they worked on a dream. That dream was to provide a place where mothers and children would not be separated because of HIV.

Nkosi's Haven is a foundation that funds homes where mothers with HIV can live and raise their children. The first Nkosi's Haven opened with ten mothers and their children. In an effort to raise awareness about HIV and AIDS, Nkosi expressed his beliefs in his 2000 speech. Nkosi said, "Care for us and accept us—we are all human beings. We are normal. We have hands. We have feet. We can walk, we can talk, we have needs just like everyone else. Don't be afraid of us—we are all the same."[17] AIDS took Nkosi's life on June 1, 2001. However, in his lifetime, he touched millions of people, and helped families remain together through a devastating disease.

However, public outrage over the issue of money versus lives made the drug companies back down and stop fighting the lawsuit.[18] Even with lower manufacturing costs, medicine is still expensive. Getting the drugs to the people who need them takes still more money and coordinated efforts.

Another program is the Mother-to-Child-Transmission (MTCT) plan that is in place in eight African nations. The program's goal is to provide the necessary drugs to prevent transmission from the mother to the baby during pregnancy, labor, delivery, and nursing, and to provide education on preventing transmission to others.[19] The program does not offer continuing antiretroviral therapy to the mothers, but it is a beginning. Reducing the rates to transmission from mothers to children is a step forward. Because the program does not offer long-term continuing medical support, the children of these women will still become orphans. Other programs are needed to assist in long-term care. One effect of the program is that it opens the lines of communication about AIDS and has helped reduce stigmas attached to those with the virus.[20]

Companies are also getting involved. Some large corporations, for example, provide their workers with education about the disease. They also offer medical support for those who are already infected. Despite the costs of these programs, the long-term benefits may outweigh the initial costs. Replacing workers requires hiring and training. Some companies in sub-Saharan Africa hire two to three people for every position because the rate of death from AIDS is so high. This process ensures that there are backup workers available when someone dies from AIDS and reduces the costs involved with hiring and training people over and over.[21]

One mining company in Johannesburg determined the cost of doing nothing about the problem and started a program for their workers. The program costs less than half of the estimated monetary losses from doing nothing. They provide their workers with information on prevention and living with HIV/AIDS as well as ongoing care and support. The company focuses on prevention, but offers confidential testing and support to its employees. While the program is expensive in the short term, it will save the company a lot of money over the next few years.[22]

In 2001, the secretary-general of the United Nations, Kofi Annan (of Ghana) addressed United Nations members stating:

> In much of Africa, AIDS is now far more than a health crisis. It has become not only the primary cause of death, but the biggest development challenge—and the same may soon be true in several Asian countries, too. At present, I am making this challenge my personal priority.[23]

He proposed the creation of the Global Fund to Fight AIDS, Tuberculosis and Malaria to help developing nations obtain the money needed to fight the AIDS crisis. The year before, he had written a report on the need of the United Nations to act on behalf of the AIDS crisis. The "Call to Action" included a five-point plan to help developing countries combat AIDS. While it took some time for the fund to develop, it did so in early 2002. The creation of the Global Fund is one way that the United Nations is working to fight the HIV/AIDS crisis around the world.

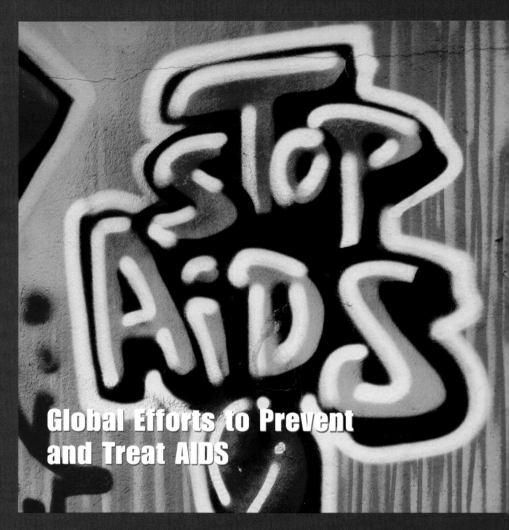

Global Efforts to Prevent and Treat AIDS

8

Across the globe, governments and humanitarian organizations are working to fight the AIDS crisis. Many public and private groups are involved. On a global scale, the United Nations is working to prevent and treat further spread of the disease. As of 2005, the United Nations consisted of 191 members, of which the United States was one.[1]

The creation of the Global Fund to Fight AIDS, Tuberculosis and Malaria was a big step in addressing the issue, although it is not yet enough. The Global Fund was created in 2002 during a United Nations meeting to raise funds to pay for programs that address these diseases. The governments of many different countries supply money for the fund. The fund does not directly run programs itself, but it does monitor the programs that it supports. A program that receives money from the Global Fund must specifically state its plans for the money and provide regular updates to show that it is being spent according to that plan. Since it began, the fund has raised $8.6 billion for use through 2008.[2] However, more money is needed to keep the fund going and to maintain the progress already made. Former South African president Nelson Mandela said in September 2005 that it is a "crying shame" that only half the money for the Global Fund's needs for 2006 and 2007 had been collected.[3]

In June 2005, the United Nations announced that the AIDS pandemic is moving faster than the means to stop it. The epidemic has not been reversed. Only 12 percent of those who need treatment worldwide receive it.[4] Who is working to improve the odds?

United Nations Programs

The following programs are sponsored by the UN to fight HIV/AIDS globally.

UNAIDS. UNAIDS is the abbreviated name for the Joint United Nations Programme on HIV/AIDS. Its mission is "preventing transmission of HIV, providing care and support, reducing the vulnerability of individuals and communities to HIV/AIDS, and alleviating the impact of the epidemic."[5] In other words, UNAIDS works to address all aspects of the epidemic, not only prevention or treatment. According to a UNAIDS publication, the organization seeks to address the global issue through the following:

- Leadership and advocacy

- Strategic information

- Tracking, monitoring, and evaluation

Since the Global Fund to Fight AIDS, Tuberculosis and Malaria was founded in 2002, it has raised $8.6 billion—but more is needed to keep the fund going and maintain the progress already made.

- Civil society engagement and the development of strategic partnerships

- Mobilization of resources[6]

The organization was founded in 1996. In 2001, the United Nations held a general assembly to discuss the AIDS pandemic. According to the organization, "Nearly two-thirds of all new infections expected this decade could be prevented by broadening existing prevention interventions to those who need them."[7] The funding to fight global AIDS through the program reached $6.1 billion in 2004.[8] Ten United Nations organizations work together to combat the problem. These include:

Office of the United Nations High Commissioner for Refugees
United Nations Children's Fund (UNICEF)
World Food Programme
United Nations Development Programme
United Nations Population Fund
United Nations Office on Drugs and Crime
International Labour Organization
United Nations Educational, Scientific and Cultural Organization (UNESCO)
World Health Organization (WHO)
The World Bank

(Information on all of these organizations can be found at the UN Web site.)

UNAIDS addresses both additional funding and coordinated efforts to reach those in need. Obtaining the money needed is an ongoing issue. Using the resources in the best possible way is also a priority. Even if money were not a problem, the way in which help is provided needs to be efficient and effective. That is, it needs to help as many people as possible as simply and quickly as possible. UNAIDS is working on both of these issues.

The work conducted by UNAIDS is at the country level whenever feasible. This means that the organization targets each country's specific needs. Programs geared this way are more effective than general programs that may or may not be useful to a specific region. This demonstrates how the organization seeks to use funding in the best possible way. For example, in sub-Saharan Africa, where HIV/AIDS is a big concern, UNAIDS helps different countries within the region address

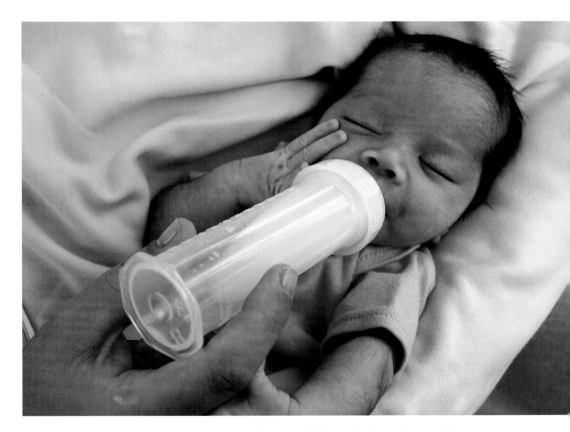

Since HIV can be passed from mother to child at birth or through breast-feeding, bottle feeding is one way of reducing transmission of the virus.

their particular needs. In Ghana, an ongoing program to monitor the effects of HIV/AIDS is continuing, whereas in Angola, UNAIDS is working with the World Bank and the Angolan government to establish a Monitoring and Evaluation Partnership Council.[9] These monitoring programs can help UNAIDS, governments, and other organizations determine the best way to deal with the HIV/AIDS situation in each country.

World Health Organization. WHO is the United Nations health agency. It works as a member of UNAIDS in addressing the global AIDS problem. The goal of WHO is "the attainment by all peoples of the highest possible level of health," which is "a state of complete physical, mental and social well-being and not merely the absence of disease or infirmity."[10] WHO's role in working with UNAIDS is to help the efforts in addressing the epidemic. It is the organizing agency for HIV/AIDS treatment, care, and support and preventing the mother-to-child transmission of HIV.

WHO has played a large role in the "3 by 5" program. The goal of this program was to treat 3 million people with HIV/AIDS by 2005. A report issued in June 2005 said that great progress had been made. The number of people treated with antiretroviral therapy had more than doubled, from 400,000 people to 1 million. However, the "3 by 5" program was not completely successful in meeting its goal. Next steps include reviewing what works and what does not and making the right adjustments in order to treat more of those in need.[11]

UNICEF. The United Nations Children's Fund, UNICEF, works specifically with children, adolescents, and families. Its role in the HIV/AIDS crisis has many parts. It works with orphaned children, helps prevent mother-to-child transmission, and educates young people on preventive measures.

UNICEF is guided by the principles outlined in the Convention on the Rights of the Child, an agreement sponsored by the UN. The Convention says: "Children have the right to develop physically, mentally and socially to their fullest potential and to express opinions freely."[12]

All members of the UN have ratified, or signed, the convention except for the United States and Somalia. Both countries have said they intend to sign. (One of the reasons the United States has not signed is the way the government is set up, with each state making its own rules on many issues that are addressed in the Convention. There is currently no time frame by which the United States will sign the Convention.)

HIV/AIDS is a primary focus for UNICEF. It works to persuade governments to treat the disease as a national emergency because of the drastic affects is has on youth. For example, in 2002, over half the 5 million new infections were among young people. People under the age of twenty-five account for more than a third of all those living with HIV/AIDS, and of those, almost two-thirds are female.[13]

UNICEF works with government, nonprofit organizations, religious groups, and youth organizations. It relies on donations for almost one third of its budget. Occasionally this can hamper the goals in some areas. UNICEF cannot hand out condoms (as of 2003), for example, because the U.S. government and the Vatican do not like the idea of a children's organization distributing them.[14]

UNICEF's priority areas include preventing new infections among young people, preventing parent-to-child transmission, and expanding and protecting orphans, vulnerable children, and families living with HIV/AIDS.[15] Multiple programs and organizations in 157 countries are involved in reaching these goals.

Other Organizations

In addition to the UN, there are a number of organizations, governmental and nongovernmental, that have joined in the AIDS fight on a worldwide scale.

Participants at a UN press conference from South Africa and Thailand speak to journalists about efforts to address the AIDS crisis. The UN has a number of programs to prevent and treat the disease.

USAID. In 1961, President John F. Kennedy established the U.S. Agency for International Development, or USAID. It is a federal agency with offices around the world. It supports the U.S. foreign policy goals of "expanding democracy and free markets while improving the lives of the citizens of the developing world."[16] The organization provides humanitarian assistance and promotes economic growth, agriculture and trade, global health, democracy, and conflict prevention. It works with both government and private organizations.

USAID supports four global regions: sub-Saharan Africa, Asia and the Near East, Latin America and the Caribbean, and Europe and Eurasia. Most of these areas have a severe

HIV/AIDS crisis. Working on the crisis is a primary activity within the organization.

The World Bank. The World Bank is not a bank in the common sense. It is two institutions owned by 184 countries. These are the International Bank for Reconstruction and Development and the International Development Association. The purpose of the World Bank is to provide financial and technical assistance to developing countries. This includes financial support in the form of low-interest loans and grants to develop educational, health, infrastructure, and communications programs, among others.[17] The World Bank monitors the HIV/AIDS crisis around the world and recognizes not only the economic impact of the disease, but the human toll as well. One of its primary goals is to combat the HIV/AIDS pandemic. Grants are provided to help reach these goals. The World Bank is actively involved in a number of regions in the prevention, education, and treatment of HIV/AIDS and related problems.

Academic Alliance for AIDS Care. This relatively new organization was founded in 2003 to address the problems in Uganda. It is made up of academic professionals in Africa and North America, the pharmaceutical industry, and other organizations.

Obstacles to Overcome

Many other organizations exist around the world. These include both governmental and private organizations, some of which work together. Some specialize in certain aspects of disease treatment or prevention. Others focus on certain geographical areas. One area that most organizations tend to agree on is that the fight against HIV/AIDS is multidimensional. That is, no one particular approach will solve the problem. A combination of education, prevention, and treatment options is necessary to effectively deal with the situation.

No one program has been able to completely address the AIDS crisis. However, some programs are making progress, such as the one in Uganda. To treat the disease effectively, a number of issues come into play. Aside from funding problems, programs need to be put into place in a way that helps those in need, which can be difficult in developing countries. A lack of education, limited medical personnel, and large geographical areas are just some of the problems that get in the way of well-meaning programs. Human behavior is also a factor. While the HIV/AIDS crisis is a community, cultural, and global problem on all different levels, it begins with individuals. This means that people need information and tools. Other factors, such as religious beliefs, are also an issue. Some religions do not support the use of condoms, for example. For many women and girls, refusing sex or asking their husbands to use a condom could result in physical assault. Drug users may understand the importance of using clean tools, but may not care when under the influence of alcohol or drugs, or when getting high is more important in the short term. Addiction is a powerful thing to overcome. Pregnant women may not even know that transmission to their babies is preventable. A number of other barriers exist that need to be addressed before programs can succeed.

Overcoming Discrimination. Across the globe, people who are infected with HIV/AIDS face discrimination. An HIV InSite report states:

> The virus continues to be marked by discrimination against population groups: those who live on the fringes of society or who are assumed to be at risk of infection because of behaviors, race, ethnicity, sexual orientation, gender, or social characteristics that are stigmatized in a particular society.[18]

In the United States, the AIDS epidemic began in the homosexual population. In other parts of the world, users of injected drugs were among the first to show signs of the disease. Now, the primary method of transmission worldwide is sexual contact. While heterosexual sex is the most common transmission method, discrimination results from beliefs that immoral people—such as sex workers and people who have multiple partners—have the disease. In India, even health care workers discriminate against patients, which makes treatment of the people and the problem even more difficult. The disease is also viewed as something that affects the poor and uneducated. While this is true in many ways, the belief that it affects only these people is not true. It also puts those in poverty even further from the help they need.

Incorrect Information. Many myths about HIV/AIDS are out there. Some people believe that it is only transmitted through certain sexual behaviors or that there is a cure. Young people, a high-risk population, tend to feel that they are invincible and that it will not happen to them. This type of thinking is extremely dangerous, in that it contributes both to contracting and to spreading the disease. In parts of Africa, especially in rural areas, people are given incorrect information by people who are highly uninformed. In recent years, for example, a number of child rapes were reported because some men were told that having sex with a virgin would cure them of AIDS.[19]

Strategy Problems. Not everyone agrees on the best way to educate people about and prevent HIV infection. One controversy that has arisen is over abstinence-only programs. These programs, particularly the one supported by President Bush's administration, promote abstinence for young people. The idea is that people should delay sexual activity for as long as possible, preferably until marriage. If both parties have been abstinent until marriage, they will not carry HIV and infect each other. If one or both partners have been sexually active, there is a chance of risk. Abstinence-only programs also promote the idea of faithfulness, or being monogamous, within marriage. If one or both parties in a marriage have sexual contact with someone outside of the marriage, both people in the marriage are at risk.

Many religious groups across the globe have viewed the promotion of condom use as the promotion of illicit sex. Even before the HIV/AIDS crisis, many religious groups (such as the Roman Catholic Church) were against the use of condoms because they oppose all forms of birth control. In addition, many religious groups feel strongly that abstinence is the best way to prevent both unwanted pregnancies and sexually transmitted diseases. In the early days of the AIDS epidemic, officials of the Catholic Church publicly said that condoms were not condoned, even for preventing the spread of HIV. More recently, however, the church has changed its position because the spread of the disease is so devastating. The church still holds that condom use is morally wrong, but recent statements

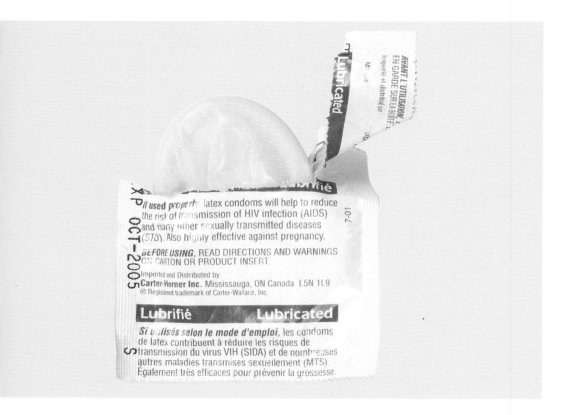

Though condoms have traditionally been opposed by some religious and cultural groups, some of this opposition has waned in view of the fact that condom use is one of the few ways to prevent the spread of HIV/AIDS.

from the church indicate that condoms could be "a last resort in battling AIDS."[20]

In 2004, a Dutch cardinal expressed the viewpoint that when a person with HIV knowingly has sex without a condom, it is also a violation of the Fifth Commandment, which states: "You shall not kill." The Catholic Church teaches that married couples should not use contraceptives. However, when one partner is HIV positive, condoms are not used to prevent pregnancy, but to prevent a life-threatening illness.[21]

The ABC program, which has been used in Uganda and is supported by the U.S. government, promotes **A**bstinence, **B**eing faithful, and using **C**ondoms—in that order—for preventing the spread of HIV/AIDS. The program stresses abstinence until marriage. Once married or in a committed relationship, couples need to be faithful. This keeps both partners from exposure to HIV transmission through sexual contact. For those who are neither abstinent nor in a committed relationship, consistent and correct condom use is necessary to help prevent HIV transmission. While it is true that abstinence will prevent the sexual transmission of the disease, critics argue that it may not be realistic. These critics argue that this concept does not guarantee protection because people who have been sexually active may not know they are infected. Moreover, these programs do not protect people who do not have much control over their situations. This includes people in abusive relationships and young women who are forced into marriage, are taught to obey men, or are victims of sexual assault.[22]

It may not be possible for everyone to be faithful or to be certain that their sexual partners are. Condoms, then, provide one method of having sex safely. The type of condom used is important. It must be one made of latex or rubber. Those made from animal skins do not prevent the disease. In addition, people must know how to use them correctly and use them at the correct times. A condom must be used for all sexual contact, including oral sex.

Although the ABC program has been successful in Uganda, some experts claim that it is not the only reason Uganda has had success in preventing the disease. They also say that how the ABC program is defined makes a difference. Writer Kavitha Rajagopalan cites the explanation of one behavioral scientist: "The various programs to combat the spread of HIV/AIDS . . . define 'abstinence' differently, and recommend it in different degrees for different groups."[23] For example, one group of people may say that abstinence means no sexual activity at all. Another may say that it means no vaginal penetration. Oral sex, then, becomes a concern for the second group. In this sense of the word, abstinence would not prevent the spread of HIV infection. In one survey, the Kaiser Family Foundation and *Seventeen* magazine found that half of those aged fifteen to seventeen said that a person who has had oral sex but not intercourse is still a virgin.[24] This indicates that some teens may put themselves or others at risk if they engage in oral sex under the belief that they are safe because they are abstaining from intercourse.

Rajagopalan also notes that abstinence is overstated as the key to Uganda's success. Behavior changed in all three areas of ABC. However, a significant amount of global AIDS funding is targeted specifically for abstinence-only programs.[25] The United States is one such example, with one third of U.S. assistance designed for abstinence-only programs. However, the United States typically does not state specifically what constitutes abstinence, and therefore it leaves people at risk who think that such behaviors as oral sex are safe.[26] This means less funding for programs that promote responsible condom use. It also makes a political and moral statement about what the United States is willing to spend money on. In Uganda, increased condom use contributed to the success of the total ABC program.[27] A report

Celebrities and AIDS

Since the early years of AIDS, celebrities have been involved in raising awareness about the illness and helping to raise funds. In the early days of the disease, some famous people died from it, including actor Rock Hudson, rock singer Freddie Mercury of Queen, and tennis player Arthur Ashe.

From concerts to other promotional events and tours, celebrities have helped bring AIDS awareness to the public. Bono, lead singer of the rock band U2

(shown here with the singer Beyoncé at a children's home in South Africa), has been involved with numerous programs to fight HIV/AIDS as well as other issues stemming from world poverty. Recently, "ONE: The Campaign to Make Poverty History" brought together a number of celebrities to help fight world poverty and HIV/AIDS. In a March 2006 Web release, the organization enlisted Tom Hanks, George Clooney, Jamie Foxx, Cameron Diaz, Penelope Cruz, Brad Pitt, Gwen Stefani, Dave Matthews, Coldplay, Sean "P. Diddy" Combs, 50 Cent, and Bono to reach millions of online viewers.[28]

published by the Guttmacher Institute notes: "To date, no educational program focusing exclusively on abstinence has shown success in delaying sexual activity."[29] Thus, some type of educational information should be in place for those who do choose to engage in sexual activity. However, if the funding is not available, this becomes yet another obstacle.

Violence Against Women. In many parts of the world, including areas where the disease is at its worst, women are largely controlled by the men in society. This is a crucial issue, as globally the number of women with HIV is growing rapidly. For many of these women, saying no to sex or using a condom are not options. Some are married and have husbands who will not agree. Others use sex in order to survive, whether it is sex for money or sex for basic needs such as food and shelter, and their partners will not use condoms.

Regarding President Bush's ABC plan and the religious agenda behind it, one writer explains that in many parts of the world, violence and forced sex between minors and adults are often the norm. The writer notes: "In these settings, A-B-C is an ideal that cannot be attained, however much politicians might wish to shroud their argument in moral terms."[30] Overcoming these types of obstacles is not easy.

Lack of Communication. The very nature of HIV/AIDS makes some people very uncomfortable. This is because talking about the disease means talking about sex. This topic is one that is historically steeped in controversy, religious beliefs, and political beliefs. Around the world, it is a touchy subject. If government officials, political figures, and religious leaders are unwilling to talk openly about sex, then getting correct information to the general population can be extremely challenging. This is one area where the government in Uganda has excelled. Political figures, religious leaders, and representatives from various organizations have been willing to talk about sex and how it relates to HIV transmission. It may be an uncomfortable topic for many, but it is an essential one, as the primary method of HIV transmission worldwide is through sex.

HIV Testing. The nature of the disease makes testing for HIV problematic: Years can elapse between the time of infection and the time that symptoms show up. This is when the disease spreads. Many people do not even know they are infected, so they take no action to prevent transmission.

Human Behavior. Changing the course of HIV/AIDS means changing what people believe and how they act. Even in life-and-death situations, this is not always an easy task. To say that abstinence is the best preventive measure is, many believe, too simplistic. People are not going to stop having sex. In addition, while using a condom is the best preventive measure for those who are sexually active, getting people to use them (and use them correctly) is another obstacle. In addition, since the disease itself is often not evident for many years after exposure, immediate interests often seem more important than long-term consequences. Programs that address human behaviors in an understanding and effective way will be more successful in creating change.

Change in teen behavior is a global concern. Susan Hunter writes: "Change in teen norms is vital to stop HIV spread because the majority of new infections occur in young people."[31] Teens are more likely to think that they are not at risk and to engage in dangerous behavior. In Uganda, teens delayed having sex in response to the AIDS crisis, which helped the problem there. The fifteen- to twenty-four-year-old group is of particularly high risk, and of those, females are showing the highest rate of new infections.

Barriers in addition to discrimination, incorrect information, testing problems, and the others discussed previously also exist. These include simple geography. Many parts of the world where HIV/AIDS is prevalent are vast geographic regions. Reaching those most in need involves extensive and difficult travel. This means that getting the necessary resources to those in need, from drugs to medical personnel, is a challenge.

The Cost of HIV/AIDS

HIV/AIDS is expensive, and the costs come in many forms. From the loss of human life to the cost of drugs and medical treatment, people are paying for the disease in many ways. Unfortunately, a large part of treating the pandemic comes down to money and resources.

The cost of antiretroviral drugs can range from a few hundred dollars per person per year to several thousand. The average cost is dropping because of the availability of generic drugs, however. These drugs can now be made available for less than $300 a year. While this is a great starting point, when multiplied by millions, the costs continue to add up. As noted earlier, even the cost of providing condoms can reach millions of dollars.

Other costs directly associated with programs include educational materials, human resources, and medical treatment. Many people in parts of the world are illiterate, which means educating them about HIV/AIDS through other means than printed materials. In addition, TVs, radios, and other forms of media are often not available. Further, some people are very wary of outsiders and may not believe what they are hearing unless it comes from a trusted source.

The cost of AIDS also comes in the form of lost work. Those most often infected are the working population. With drastic reductions in the workforce, an economy slows down and can even collapse. The economic impact of AIDS could be disastrous worldwide if the epidemic is not addressed.

Other costs of HIV/AIDS come in the form of helping those who survive. Children and the elderly are left behind with no one to care for them. The millions of AIDS orphans require social help; if it is not provided, an extremely unstable environment could result.

In *Global AIDS: Myths and Facts*, the writers say that recent evidence shows that treating AIDS saves health systems money in the end. They note that the initial costs for antiretroviral drugs is considerable, but that the use of these drugs in the United States, Europe, Canada, and Brazil has reduced costs by averting the need for more expensive types of care, including long hospital stays and treatments for opportunistic infections. For instance, the Brazilian Ministry of Health estimated that the use of medications eliminated the need for more than 250,000 hospital admissions between 1997 and 2000.[32]

The Costs to Come

AIDS expert Susan Hunter writes: "Large-scale prevention demands a huge investment of time, money, and commitment by individuals, communities, businesses, and government."[33] The creation of the Global Fund was a step toward a solution. However, the funding currently available falls short of what is actually needed. In 2002, global spending on the crisis reached $2.8 billion. What was needed was more than three times that amount—$9.2 billion. In 2007, an estimated $15 billion will be required, and $25 billion will be needed by 2025.[34]

The United States and the Fight Against AIDS

In January 2003, President George W. Bush promised $15 billion in funding to fight HIV/AIDS on a global scale. This was made official in May 2003 when Congress approved the United States Leadership Against HIV/AIDS, Tuberculosis and Malaria Act of 2003. The HIV/AIDS program, which sprang from the 2003 act, is called the President's Emergency Plan for AIDS Relief (PEPFAR). The plan is designed to take place over a five-year period, with $3 billion spent each year. This is dependent on how much Congress approves each year, however, so the number could be more or less. The goal is to have 2 million people taking antiretroviral medicines by 2008, to prevent 7 million new infections, and to care for 10 million people who are infected with HIV or have been orphaned by AIDS.[1]

The plan provided $2.8 billion in 2005, and this increased to $3.2 billion in 2006. President Bush requested more than $4 billion for 2007. The program works with partner organizations. In 2005, over 80 percent of those organizations were indigenous, meaning that they were local. This is important because local organizations are in a better position to help people. The program also gave $75.6 million to programs promoting abstinence and fidelity (remaining faithful to one sexual partner) in 2005. Funds to supply condoms and "related activities" totaled $65.7 million in 2005.[2]

In a February 2006 update, the Office of the U.S. Global AIDS Coordinator published a report on progress. At that time, the program had provided antiretroviral treatment to more than 401,000 men, women, and children in the fifteen focus countries. Of those receiving treatment, 60 percent were female.[3]

Despite the number of people reached by the program, and despite the fact that it is "the largest international health initiative in history by a government dedicated to a single disease,"[4] the program has still received criticism. One concern is that the majority of funds are designated for treating those who are already infected. While this is certainly a priority, some people feel that more needs to be spent on prevention efforts.

Some people oppose the fact that the funds spent to treat those infected are spent on brand-name drugs manufactured by United States pharmaceutical companies. The World Health Organization supports the use of generic drugs.[5] Generic drugs use the same formulas as the originals, so there is no difference between a generic drug and the brand-name drug aside from the price. International laws governing pharmaceutical drugs and who owns the rights to make drugs complicate the process. Large manufacturers who keep the rights to make certain drugs say that the reason the costs of the drugs are high is to cover the costs of research and manufacturing. However, not everyone agrees with this. A report produced by AVERT states that "much of their [pharmaceutical companies'] profits are thought to go on executive salaries, publicity, advertising, promotion, corporate sponsorship and branding, rather than [research and development]."[6]

Most funds from PEPFAR—the President's Emergency Plan for AIDS Relief—are spent to treat those already infected. Some people feel that more needs to be spent on prevention.

Further, some criticize the fact that most of the funds for prevention are limited to abstinence-only programs, which promote no sex before marriage and remaining faithful once married.[7] These people argue that the U.S. government is trying to push the ideals of the conservative right. Abstinence would in fact prevent most HIV transmission, but the strategy alone is unsuccessful.[8] People who do plan to have sex but are taught only about abstinence will not have the necessary knowledge to protect themselves. In addition, even if someone waits until marriage, he or she can still be infected by the marriage partner.[9]

Another point of contention is that the law allows for up to $1 billion to be contributed annually to the Global Fund—on the condition that other countries match the donation to ensure that the United States does not provide more than 33 percent of the total Global Fund.[10] Additionally, the United States could have simply added funds to the Global Fund rather than spending time and money setting up PEPFAR, a new organization.[11]

Finally, some people are critical over what they see as wrong priorities. They point to the huge difference between spending on military and security and spending on a major pandemic. The 2001 terrorist attacks on the United States were horrific. However, as critics point out, nearly three times as many people

UN Secretary-General Kofi Annan meets with a group of people living with AIDS. Annan has urged the United States to spend more on fighting the disease.

die every day from AIDS as were killed on September 11. They are not saying that the lives lost on September 11 were unimportant, only that there is a huge gap between funds spent fighting terrorism and the amount spent on fighting AIDS. The United States has spent hundreds of billions of dollars on the war in Iraq, projects addressing terrorism, and efforts to ensure national security, compared to a few billion on a disease that takes about eight thousand lives on a daily basis.[12] (Some estimates put the total at eighty-five hundred daily as of October 2005.[13]) United Nations Secretary-General Kofi Annan "invited the USA to match its commitment to eradicating weapons of mass destruction with a similar effort for HIV/AIDS."[14] (This statement was made before the United States determined that Iraq did not have these weapons.)

However, despite the criticisms, the United States currently spends more on fighting AIDS than any other country does. While additional funding could easily be put to good use, the funds spent thus far have reached some goals. Only time will tell the extent of the resources the U.S. government will decide to spend on the fight against this global pandemic and how these resources will be distributed.

Why Should the United States Help?

Does the United States have a responsibility to pay more than other countries? Many would argue yes. Being the wealthiest country in the world comes with responsibilities. These responsibilities include addressing major humanitarian crises, of which the HIV/AIDS pandemic is the largest in history.

Many people believe that the United States should pay much more than it is currently doing on the global AIDS crisis. Many Western countries contribute to fighting the problem, and the United States is the largest contributor. However, all the funds are still not enough to solve the problem. Oxfam International is a group of twelve organizations "working together with over 3,000 partners in more than 100 countries to find lasting solutions to poverty, suffering and injustice."[15] In commenting about U.S. spending on HIV/AIDS, a May 2006 Oxfam report states:

> Given the size of its economy, the US contribution is extremely small. The Bush Administration, which had no problem in immediately funding US $95 [million] to buy one drug (cipro) for the possible threat of anthrax when 18 people were infected, seems to have a great problem donating more than US $500 [million] to the [Global] Fund for three diseases that kill five million every year. A fairer and more generous contribution of US $4 [billion] per year based on GNP . . . would be the equivalent to the amount spent in 24 days in the USA on soft drinks, or in 14 days on fast food.[16]

Susan Hunter writes: "Currently, the United States spends

less than half a percent of its GDP on all foreign aid, the lowest of any developed country."[17] (GDP stands for gross domestic product, the value of goods and services of a country. GNP, or gross national product, is the GDP plus income earned abroad.) A 2005 survey indicated that most people in the Western world believe that the United States is spending too little on the AIDS crisis and that increased spending will make a difference.[18] This included people living in the United States. Additionally, people in several other countries responded that the United States is giving too little in the fight against HIV/AIDS. The percentages of those with this belief are as follows:

Canada: 48 percent
France: 52 percent
Germany: 48 percent
Great Britain: 57 percent
Italy: 38 percent
Japan: 7 percent (79 percent responded "don't know")[19]

In comparison with twenty-one other countries, the United States spent the lowest total percentage of GNP in 2000.[20] In other words, even though the United States spends the most in total dollars, it is well below what other countries spend in terms of money available.

Perhaps the best reason the United States should consider increased funding is that it is the moral thing to do. Millions of people are affected by HIV/AIDS. These people are not simply those who are infected and their immediate families. In some very basic terms, the HIV/AIDS crisis affects everyone on a global scale, including people in the United States.

AIDS experts Alexander Irwin, Joyce Millen, and Dorothy Fallows outline a number of ways the AIDS crisis affects the United States (and others) in their book *Global AIDS: Myths and Facts*. In addition to the moral argument (which they say is

Magic's Mission

Earvin "Magic" Johnson was at the top of his game when he was diagnosed with HIV in 1991. A basketball superstar, he had won numerous awards and set a number of records on the court. At the time of his diagnosis, many people considered the disease to be one that mostly affected white, homosexual males. Johnson is an African-American heterosexual male. Soon after his diagnosis, he started educating people, particularly youths, about safe sex. In a June 2002 interview, Johnson is quoted as saying,

> Young people want you to be real with them. If you tell them the real story, what happened, why it happened, then they're going to listen. So I just try to be direct.[21]

Johnson officially retired in 1991, but returned to the basketball court a few times after that. However, his mission in life became one of AIDS awareness. He founded the Magic Johnson Foundation in December 1991 to help serve underprivileged youths. The foundation also contributes to HIV awareness and prevention programs. The organization has donated between $5 and $10 million to AIDS organizations.[22]

Thanks to a healthy lifestyle and the available HIV medications, Magic Johnson is still doing well. He lives with his wife and children and continues his work in helping others and raising awareness about the disease.

the most compelling reason the United States should do more), they note other reasons that can have more influence on those who believe that the crisis does not affect them personally.

First, they explain that the HIV/AIDS crisis is a threat to anyone traveling or working in high-risk areas. As discussed earlier in this book, it did not take long for the virus to travel across the globe. Second, they explain that the crisis will have an economic impact, not only on the countries affected, but also on companies with global interests. They write: "Major international companies doing business in regions with high HIV-prevalence are increasingly concerned about the effects of AIDS on productivity and profitability."[23] The HIV/AIDS crisis also creates a security issue. In countries that are hit hard, military forces are diminished as well. With the rising number of orphans and others left without direction, the result could be a very unstable society.[24]

Again, the most important reason is that wealth should not determine who deserves to live and who dies. The authors write: "Human beings with identical medical conditions are enabled to live—or condemned to die—because of their income.[25] Author Greg Behrman, in his book *The Invisible People*, outlines the history of the disease and the slow response of the United States to the pandemic. In the book's introduction, he writes: "Throughout the pandemic's twenty-year flight, the United States has shrunk from its strategic imperative and its moral obligation, failing at almost every turn to lead a comprehensive global response to the pandemic." However, he also writes: "Yet, the exploration that follows has been spurred by a profound faith in the singularly American capacity to harness its unique sense of mission to achieve a transcendent aim."[26]

HIV/AIDS and Human Rights

The HIV/AIDS crisis is in many ways a human rights issue. The disease does not decide who and when it will strike. However, humans decide how and when they will respond. The fact that the disease affects developing countries the most, and that the problem is now epidemic, says something about money, politics, and power. Who decides who lives and who dies?

The United States is based on the idea of individual freedom and the power to achieve self-fulfillment. Many people take the idea of finding one's life passion, for example, for granted. However, for the millions of people simply trying to survive from one day to the next, such ideas may not seem relevant. The United States has the opportunity to do something about the HIV/AIDS pandemic, as do the other wealthy countries of the world. The PEPFAR program is a start, as is the Global Fund and the other organizations working to solve the crisis.

A 2003 report regarding U.S. global AIDS policy by the Guttmacher Institute notes: "To be sure, the stakes are high for the millions of people around the world at risk of or living with HIV or AIDS—and for the world around them."[27]

Ensuring Rights

Globally, it is everyone's responsibility to make sure that the rights of those with HIV are protected. Ensuring the health and safety of the general population needs to be balanced with proper treatment of those living with HIV/AIDS. Unfortunately, individual rights are often overlooked with the emphasis on public health. This is often fueled by incorrect information about HIV and how it spreads. From the early days of the disease, human rights issues became a focus. Many people with HIV were unable to obtain work, for example, and this problem continues today. Nearly twenty years later, many people are discriminated against for being HIV positive, even though transmission cannot occur through casual contact. Views about what types of people are infected and incorrect information allow this discrimination to continue.

In 1948, the United Nations drafted the "Universal Declaration of Human Rights." The declaration lists thirty articles that outline basic human rights. Some of these include the following:

- Everyone has the right to a standard of living adequate for the health and well-being of himself and of his family, including food, clothing, housing and medical care and necessary social services, and the right to security in the event of unemployment, sickness, disability, widowhood, old age or other lack of livelihood in circumstances beyond his control.

- Motherhood and childhood are entitled to special care and assistance. All children, whether born in or out of wedlock, shall enjoy the same social protection.

- Everyone, without any discrimination, has the right to equal pay for equal work.[28]

These are but a few of the rights listed that can be directly applied to the HIV/AIDS crisis. Additional rights have been outlined in a number of treaties. Two that have direct impact on HIV/AIDS are the Convention on the Elimination of All Forms of Discrimination Against Women and the Convention on the Rights of the Child. Human rights and HIV/AIDS are closely connected because those infected are vulnerable and often treated poorly. This includes men, women, and children. However, some populations, such as women and children, are more vulnerable than others. AIDS experts Sofia Gruskin and Daniel Tarantola write: "Adolescent girls and boys may be vulnerable to HIV by being denied access to preventive information, education, and services."[29] Further, it is the government's responsibility to guarantee the rights of its citizens, which, in the case of HIV/AIDS, includes access to information. According to Gruskin and Tarantola, "A state has to ensure, for example, that religious groups are not successful when they try to stop adolescents from accessing reproductive health information."[30] Racism, gender-based discrimination, and homophobia continue to threaten the rights of those infected with HIV.

Providing the necessary information and treatment to those who need it is a basic part of human rights. This would also lead to more effective means of addressing the problem. Unfortunately, this is not always the case. Gruskin and Tarantola conclude: "The importance of bringing HIV/AIDS policies and programs in line with international human rights law is generally acknowledged but, unfortunately, rarely carried out in reality."[31]

The Future of AIDS

In June 2006, people around the world observed the twenty-five year mark of the HIV/AIDS crisis. During those years, what started as a few cases of a strange disease grew into a worldwide pandemic. While the overall transmission rates of HIV have slowed or reversed in some areas, such as in developed nations, transmission rates are still rising in many developing countries. Drug companies continue to research ways for treating the disease, but there is no cure for HIV.

How the HIV/AIDS crisis unfolds from here depends on a number of factors. Funding is a major issue, and one that will need to be assessed on an ongoing basis. From there, reality-based programs that work, rather than those based on biases or ideal situations, need to be put in place in efficient ways. The crisis can worsen and lead to the frightening numbers now predicted. Or, it might stay about the same, without rapid growth, but without a decrease in numbers.

Obviously, the best situation is one where the number of predicted infections does not occur. Ideally, antiretroviral medications would be made available to all those who need them, and further infections would be prevented through the methods outlined in this book. This, combined with a vaccine, would be a perfect solution. However, a vaccine is still many years off, and something needs to be done in the meantime to slow the epidemic.

Although the current and estimated numbers are staggering, hope still exists. United Nations Secretary-General Kofi Annan said in June 2005 that it could be possible to stop the cycle of new HIV infections and AIDS.[1] This requires more funding and resources from traditional donors, private sectors, and the affected countries. There are some encouraging signs.

Ways to Get Involved

It can be overwhelming to think about the huge numbers of people affected by HIV/AIDS. One person may feel that he or she has nothing to offer. However, this is not the case. Over the past two decades, the actions of AIDS activists and individuals have made great strides in fighting the epidemic.

One of the first things young people can do is become educated. Only with accurate information can the disease be prevented and fought. Knowing as much as possible will not only help individuals, but also help people see what needs to be done from here. A number of resources exist that provide thorough, accurate information. Many are geared specifically toward adolescents. When myths are separated from facts, people can become empowered. The Student Global AIDS

Students take part in a candlelight vigil to raise awareness about HIV/AIDS. Concerned activists can make a huge difference in how this crisis is handled.

Campaign is one organization that specifically targets high school and college students.

Other ways young people can get involved is to lobby politicians and help raise money for organizations working on the AIDS crisis. Even though young people cannot yet vote, they can make their voices heard through letters to newspapers and magazines and letters to politicians. Getting involved with local groups that are raising money and awareness about the HIV/AIDS crisis is another way to help that is easy to do.

Finally, practicing compassion for those affected is a great way to make a difference, one person or one group at a time. HIV/AIDS affects people from all walks of life: all races, backgrounds, professions, gender, and age. The disease does not discriminate; neither should we.

Chapter Notes

Chapter 2 What Is AIDS?

1. "The HIV Life Cycle," *AIDSMeds.com*, June 4, 2000, <http://www.aidsmeds.com/lessons/LifeCycleIntro.htm> (September 18, 2005).

2. Hung Y. Fan, Ross F. Conner, and Luis P. Villarreal, *AIDS: Science and Society*, 4th ed. (Sudbury, Mass.: Jones and Bartlett Publishers, 2004), pp. 42–44.

3. Ibid., p. 45.

4. Ibid., p. 46.

5. "The Immune System," *NIAID NetNews*, n.d., <http://www.niaid.nih.gov/final/immun/immun.htm> (September 18, 2005).

6. Ken R. Wells and Teresa G. Odle, "AIDS tests," *Gale Encyclopedia of Medicine* (Detroit: Thomson Gale, 2006).

7. Centers for Disease Control and Prevention, "Living with HIV/AIDS," September 2005, <http://www.cdc.gov/hiv/pubs/brochure/livingwithhiv.htm> (June 25, 2006).

8. Darrell E. Ward, *The AmFAR AIDS Handbook* (New York: W. W. Norton & Company, 1999), pp. 51–54.

9. Alexander Irwin, Joyce Millen, and Dorothy Fallows, *Global AIDS: Myths and Facts; Tools for Fighting the AIDS Pandemic* (Cambridge, Mass.: South End Press, 2003), p. xxv.

10. Ward, p. 55.

11. Ibid., pp. 55–56.

12. Ibid., pp. 35–48.

13. Ibid., p. 37.

14. Ibid., pp. 37–38.

15. Ibid., p. 418.

16. "How HIV Is Spread," San Francisco AIDS Foundation, April 14, 2006, <http://www.sfaf.org/aids101/transmission.html#possibly_infectious> (June 5, 2006).

17. Ibid.

18. Ibid.

19. Rebecca J. Frey and Teresa G. Odle, "AIDS," *Gale Encyclopedia of Medicine* (Detroit: Thomson Gale, 2006).

20. Ward, pp. 45–46.

21. "How HIV Is Spread."

22. Ibid.

Chapter 3 History of the Disease

1. "The origins of HIV and the first cases of AIDS," *Avert.org*, July 26, 2005, <http://www.avert.org/origins.htm> (September 18, 2005).

2. Ibid.

3. Ibid.

4. Ibid.

5. Jaap Goudsmit, *Viral Sex: The Nature of AIDS* (New York: Oxford University Press, 1997), pp. 25ff.

6. "The origins of HIV and the first cases of AIDS."

7. Ibid.

8. Ronald Bayer and Gerald M. Oppenheimer, *AIDS Doctors: Voices from the Epidemic* (New York: Oxford University Press, 2000), pp. 18–21.

9. Sofia Gruskin and Daniel Tarantola, "Human Rights and HIV/AIDS," *HIV InSite Knowledge Base Chapter,* April 2002, <http://hivinsite.ucsf.edu/InSite?page=kb-08-01-07> (September 27, 2005).

10. Peter J. Ungvarski and Jacquelyn Haak Flaskerud, *HIV/AIDS: A Guide to Primary Care Management* (Philadelphia, Pa.: W. B. Saunders Company, 1999), p. 2.

11. Bayer and Oppenheimer, p. 32.

12. Ungvarski and Flaskerud, p. 2.

13. "The History of AIDS, 1981–1986," *Avert.org*, May 4, 2006, <http://www.avert.org/his81_86.htm> (June 6, 2006).

14. "The History of AIDS, 1987–1992," *Avert.org*, May 2, 2006, <http://www.avert.org/his87_92.htm> (June 6, 2006).

15. "Leading the Health Sector Response to HIV/AIDS," HIV/AIDS Department, Family and Community Health Cluster, World Health Organization, September 2002, p. 2, <http://www.who.int/hiv/pub/advocacy/pub20/en/index.html> (September 20, 2006).

16. Hung Y. Fan, Ross F. Conner, and Luis P. Villarreal, *AIDS: Science and Society*, 4th ed. (Sudbury, Mass: Jones and Bartlett Publishers, 2004), p. 3.

17. "The History of AIDS, 1981–1986."

18. "About Our Work: Most At Risk Populations," Department of Health and Human Services/Centers for Disease Control and Prevention, Global AIDS Program (GAP), January 2005, <http://www.cdc.gov/nchstp/od/gap/pa_marp.htm> (June 27, 2006).

19. "HIV Infection in Adolescents and Young Adults in the U.S.," National Institutes of Health, U.S. Department of Health and Human Services, May 2006, <http://www.niaid.nih.gov/factsheets/hivadolescent.htm> (June 6, 2006).

20. Centers for Disease Control and Prevention, "Basic Statistics: AIDS Cases by Age," October 16, 2006, <http://www.cdc.gov/hiv/topics/surveillance/basic.htm#aidsage> (November 22, 2006).

21. "HIV Infection in Adolescents and Young Adults in the U.S."

22. "Population by Race and Hispanic or Latino Origin," U.S. Census Bureau, December 2000, <http://factfinder.census.gov/servlet/QTTable?_bm=n&_lang=en&qr_name=DEC_2000_SF1_U_QTP3&ds_name=DEC_2000_SF1_U&geo_id=01000US> (June 6, 2006).

23. "Black or African American Populations," CDC Office of Minority Health, May 2, 2006, <http://www.cdc.gov/omh/Populations/BAA/BAA.htm> (June 6, 2006).

24. "HIV Infection in Adolescents and Young Adults in the U.S."

25. Ibid.

26. "HIV Infection in Infants and Children," National Institutes of

Health, U.S. Department of Health and Human Services, Fact Sheet, July 2004, <http://www.niaid.nih.gov/factsheets/hivchildren.htm> (June 6, 2006).

27. Ibid.

28. "HIV Infection in Women," National Institutes of Health, U.S. Department of Health and Human Services, Fact Sheet, May 2006, <http://www.niaid.nih.gov/factsheets/womenhiv.htm> (June 6, 2006).

29. "HIV Infection in Minority Populations," National Institutes of Health, U.S. Department of Health and Human Services, Fact Sheet, April 2005, <http://www.niaid.nih.gov/factsheets/Minor.htm> (June 6, 2006).

30. Ibid.

31. Ibid.

32. "More Than a Million Americans Living with HIV," *MSNBC.com*, June 13, 2005, <http://www.msnbc.msn.com/id/8203052> (June 13, 2005).

33. Rebecca J. Frey and Teresa G. Odle, "AIDS," *Gale Encyclopedia of Medicine* (Detroit: Thomson Gale, 2006).

34. David Alain Wohl, "HIV JournalView, Top Ten Reports of 2004: AIDS Epidemic Update: December 2004, UNAIDS/WHO," The Body Pro, January 2005, <http://www.thebodypro.com/journalview/jan05.html#update> (September 24, 2005).

35. Alexander Irwin, Joyce Millen, and Dorothy Fallows, *Global AIDS: Myths and Facts; Tools for Fighting the AIDS Pandemic* (Cambridge, Mass.: South End Press, 2003), p. 2.

36. Ibid., p. 6.

Chapter 4   Treatments

1. Hung Y. Fan, Ross F. Conner, and Luis P. Villarreal, *AIDS: Science and Society*, 4th ed. (Sudbury, Mass: Jones and Bartlett Publishers, 2004), p. 46.

2. "The Stages of HIV Disease," San Francisco AIDS Foundation, April 13, 2006, <http://www.sfaf.org/aids101/hiv_disease.html> (June 6, 2006).

3. Alexander Irwin, Joyce Millen, and Dorothy Fallows, *Global AIDS: Myths and Facts; Tools for Fighting the AIDS Pandemic* (Cambridge, Mass.: South End Press, 2003), p. 74.

4. Emma Guest, *Children of AIDS: Africa's Orphan Crisis* (Sterling, Va.: Pluto Press, 2003), p. xi.

5. Fan, Conner, and Villarreal, p. 187.

6. Ibid., p. 189.

7. "AIDS Epidemic Racing Forward, Treatment-Experienced Patients Set High Goals, Hopes for Therapeutic Vaccine," *The AIDS Reader* (Darien, Conn.: CMP Media, 2005), p. 331.

8. Ibid.

9. Fan, Conner, and Villarreal, p. 184.

10. Andrew Pollack and Lawrence Altman, "Large Trial Finds AIDSVAX Vaccine Fails to Stop Infection," *The New York Times*, February 25, 2003, <http://www.hivandhepatitis.com/vaccines/022503a.html> (June 25, 2006).

12. Susan Hunter, *Black Death: AIDS in Africa* (New York: Palgrave MacMillan, 2003), p. 35.

12. "Providing drug treatment for millions," *Avert.org*, July 26, 2005, <http://www.avert.org/drugtreatment.htm> (October 1, 2005).

13. "AIDS and HIV antiretrovial drug treatment in resource poor communities," *Avert.org*, October 3, 2006, <http://www.avert.org/aidstreatment.htm> (November 18, 2006).

14. "An Exceptional Response to AIDS," Joint United Nations Programme on HIV/AIDS, n.d., <http://www.usembassy.it/pdf/other/exceptional.pdf> (June 27, 2006)

Chapter 5 AIDS in the United States

1. "United States HIV and AIDS Statistics Summary," *Avert.org*, May 15, 2005, <http://www.avert.org/statsum.htm> (June 6, 2006).

2. Ibid.

3. Ibid.

4. "HIV/AIDS Surveillance and Reporting in the United States,"

HIV InSite, February 2001, <http://hivinsite.ucsf.edu/ InSite?page=kb-08-02-02> (September 27, 2005).

5. "HIV Reporting Policy, April 2006," *Statehealthfacts.org*, June 2006, <http://www.statehealthfacts.org/cgi-bin/healthfacts.cgi? action=compare&category=HIV%2fAIDS&subcategory=HIV+ Testing&topic=State+HIV+Reporting+Policy> (June 19, 2006).

6. Ibid.

7. Ibid.

8. Mark Cichocki, "Your Guide to HIV/AIDS: Name Reporting … Good or Bad?" *About.com*, n.d., <http://aids.about.com/cs/ hivtesting/i/named-2.htm> (September 27, 2005).

9. "HIV Testing in the USA," *Avert.org*, May 25, 2006, <http://www.avert.org/hiv-testing-usa.htm> (June 19, 2006).

10. Cichocki.

11. "HIV Testing in the USA."

12. Ibid.

13. "A Glance at the HIV/AIDS Epidemic," Centers for Disease Control and Prevention, April 2006, <http://www.cdc.gov/hiv/ resources/factsheets/At-A-Glance.htm> (June 27, 2006).

14. Ibid.

15. Ibid.

16. "Basic Statistics, HIV/AIDS Diagnoses," Centers for Disease Control and Prevention, August 31, 2006, <http://www. cdc.gov/hiv/topics/surveillance/basic.htm> (September 23, 2006).

17. "A Glance at the HIV/AIDS Epidemic."

18. Ibid.

19. "Table 11: Estimated numbers of persons living with AIDS at the end of 2004, by race/ethnicity, sex, and transmission category," Centers for Disease Control and Prevention, *HIV/AIDS Surveillance Report, Volume 16, Cases of HIV Infection and AIDS in the United States, 2004,* February 1, 2006, <http://www.cdc.gov/ hiv/topics/surveillance/resources/reports/2004report/default.htm> (June 21, 2006).

20. "HIV/AIDS among women," CDC HIV/AIDS Fact Sheet, U.S. Department of Health and Human Services, April 2006.

21. "HIV/AIDS among African Americans," CDC HIV/AIDS Fact Sheet, U.S. Department of Health and Human Services, April 2006.

22. "A Glance at the HIV/AIDS Epidemic."

23. "Reported Number of AIDS Cases, Cumulative through December 2004," The Kaiser Family Foundation, n.d., <http://www.statehealthfacts.org/cgi-bin/healthfacts.cgi?action=compare& category=HIV%2fAIDS&subcategory=Cumulative+AIDS+Cases& topic+Cumulative+AIDS+Cases+All+Ages> (November 18, 2006).

24. Katy Reckdahl, "The Changing Faces of AIDS," *Gambit Weekly, The Best of New Orleans*, July 29, 2003, <http://www.bestofneworleans.com/dispatch/2003-07-29/cover_story.html> (June 27, 2006).

25. "About the CDC," Centers for Disease Control and Prevention, n.d., <http://www.cdc.gov/about/default.htm> (September 26, 2005).

26. "Advancing HIV Prevention: The Four Strategies," Centers for Disease Control and Prevention, Divisions of HIV/AIDS Prevention, July 23, 2003, <http://www.cdc.gov/hiv/partners/ahp_program.htm> (September 26, 2005).

27. "HIV/AIDS Policy Fact Sheet: U.S. Federal Funding for HIV/AIDS: The FY 2007 Budget Request," The Kaiser Foundation, February 2006, <http://www.kff.org/hivaids/upload/7029-03.pdf> (September 23, 2006).

28. "HIV/AIDS in the United States," *The Body*, June 2004, <http://www.thebody.com/aac/statefact/usa_2004.html> (September 26, 2005).

Chapter 6   AIDS Around the World

1. "Reversing the Epidemic: Facts and Policy Options," United Nations Development Programme, 2004, <http://europeandcis.undp.org/hiv/?english> (September 28, 2005).

2. "AIDS Epidemic Update: December 2005: Latin America,"

UNAIDS, 2005, <http://www.unaids.org/epi/2005/
doc/EPIupdate2005_html_en/epi05_09_en.htm> (August 24,
2006).

3. "North America, Western and Central Europe," UNAIDS, 2004,
<http:// <http://data.unaids.org/Publications/Fact-Sheets04/
FS-High-income_en.pdf> (August 28, 2006).

4. Ibid.

5. Ibid.

6. Ibid.

7. Ibid.

8. "United Kingdom HIV & AIDS Statistics Summary," *Avert.org*,
August 2, 2006, <http://www.avert.org/uksummary.htm>
(August 24, 2006).

9. "France 2004 update," UNAIDS, 2004, <http://www.who.int/
GlobalAtlas/predefinedReports/EFS2004/EFS_PDFs/EFS2004_
FR.pdf> (September 27, 2005).

10. "Spain 2004 update," UNAIDS, 2004, <http://www.who.int/
GlobalAtlas/predefinedReports/EFS2004/EFS_PDFs/EFS2004_
ES.pdf> (September 27, 2005).

11. "HIV/AIDS in Russia, Eastern Europe, and Central Asia,"
Avert.org, August 25, 2005, <http://www.avert.org/ecstatee.htm>
(September 28, 2005).

12. Alexander Irwin, Joyce Millen, and Dorothy Fallows, *Global
AIDS: Myths and Facts; Tools for Fighting the AIDS Pandemic*
(Cambridge, Mass.: South End Press, 2003), p. 7.

13. "AIDS Epidemic Update: December 2005: Eastern Europe and
Central Asia," UNAIDS, <http://www.unaids.org/epi/2005/doc/
EPIupdate2005_html_en/epi05_07_en.htm> (September 29,
2006).

14. Irwin, Millen, and Fallows, p. 7.

15. "AIDS Epidemic Update: December 2005: Eastern Europe and
Central Asia."

16. "HIV/AIDS in Russia, Eastern Europe, and Central Asia."

17. "Combating HIV/AIDS in Europe and Central Asia," The World

Bank, Global HIV/AIDS Program, Europe and Central Asia Human Development Department, Europe and Central Asia Region, 2005, p. 2, <http://www.aidsmedia.org/files/985_file_World_Bank_English.pdf> (June 27, 2006).

18. Irwin, Millen, and Fallows, p. 8.

19. "Asia," UNAIDS Fact Sheet, 2006, <http://data.unaids.org/pub/GlobalReport/2006/200605-FS_Asia_en.pdf#search=%22UNAIDS%20fact%20sheet%20asia%22> (September 23, 2006).

20. David F. Gordon, editor, "The Next Wave of HIV/AIDS: Nigeria, Ethiopia, Russia, India and China," National Intelligence Council, September 2002, p. 4, <www.odci.gov/nic> (September 20, 2006).

21. "Asia."

22. "HIV & AIDS in India," *Avert.org*, August 12, 2005, <http://www.avert.org/aidsindia.htm> (September 29, 2005).

23. Ibid.

24. "AIDS Epidemic Update: December 2005: Asia," UNAIDS/WHO, <http://www.unaids.org/epi05_06_en.pdf> (August 23, 2006).

25. Ibid.

Chapter 7 AIDS in Africa

1. Alexander Irwin, Joyce Millen, and Dorothy Fallows, *Global AIDS: Myths and Facts; Tools for Fighting the AIDS Pandemic* (Cambridge, Mass.: South End Press, 2003), p. 1.

2. "HIV and AIDS in Africa," *Avert.org*, July 26, 2005, <http://www.avert.org/aafrica.htm> (September 29, 2005).

3. Ibid.

4. Ibid.

5. Emma Guest, *Children of AIDS: Africa's Orphan Crisis* (Sterling, Va.: Pluto Press, 2003), p. 10.

6. Susan Hunter, *Black Death: AIDS in Africa* (New York: Palgrave MacMillan, 2003), p. 23.

7. "2006 Report on the Global AIDS Epidemic," UNAIDS/WHO,

2006, p. 8, <http://data.unaids.org/pub/GlobalReport/2006/2006_GR_CH02_en.pdf> (October 18, 2006).

8. Hunter, p. 44.

9. Guest, p. 10.

10. Hunter, p. 32.

11. Ibid., pp. 32–33.

12. Ibid., pp. 33.

13. "Country Profile—Uganda," Centers for Disease Control and Prevention, Global Aids Program, September 13, 2005, <http://www.cdc.gov/nchstp/od/gap/countries/uganda.htm> (September 30, 2005).

14. Ibid.

15. Hunter, p. 33.

16. "The Battle Over Uganda's AIDS Campaign," BBC News, April 12, 2005, <http://news.bbc.co.uk/2/hi/africa/4433069.stm> (June 7, 2006).

17. "About Nkosi," Nkosi's Haven Foundation, 2006, <http://nkosi.iafrica.com/contentPage.asp?pageID=5#void> (June 27, 2006).

18. Hunter, p. 35.

19. "MTCT-Plus initiative now in eight African nations: women enter program in pregnancy and continue," *AIDS Alert*, vol. 19, no. 8, August 2004, p. S2.

20. Ibid.

21. Irwin, Millen, and Fallows, p. 157.

22. Jan du Toit and Amelia Burger, "Tackling HIV/AIDS in the workplace: best practices being developed in South Africa carries an important message for companies everywhere," *European Business Forum*, no.176, Spring 2004, p. 70.

23. Kofi Annan, "Statement on the Challenge of Eradicating Poverty for Sustainable Development," Third United Nations Conference on the Least Developed Countries, May 14, 2001, <http://www.globalpolicy.org/socecon/trade/unctad/2001/anna0514.htm> (June 23, 2006).

Chapter 8   Global Efforts to Prevent and Treat AIDS

1. "Membership of Principal United Nations Organs in 2005," United Nations, n.d., <http://www.un.org/News/Press/docs/2005/org1436.doc.htm> (September 30, 2005).

2. "Who We Are and What We Do," brochure, The Global Fund to Fight AIDS, Tuberculosis and Malaria, 2005, <http://www.theglobalfund.org/en/about/publications/brochure/> (June 10, 2006).

3. "Africa: AIDS fund running dry, Mandela warns," UN Integrated Regional Informational Networks, September 27, 2005, <http://www.aegis.com/news/irin/2005/IR05964.html> (September 28, 2006).

4. "AIDS Epidemic Racing Forward, Treatment-Experienced Patients Set High Goals, Hopes for Therapeutic Vaccine," *The AIDS Reader* (Darien, Conn.: CMP Media, Inc., 2005), p. 331.

5. "What Is UNAIDS?" Joint United Nations Programme on HIV/AIDS, n.d., <http://www.unaids.org/en/about+unaids/what+is+unaids.asp> (August 24, 2006).

6. Ibid.

7. "An Exceptional Response to AIDS," UNAIDS, n.d., <http://www.usembassy.it/pdf/other/exceptional.pdf> (August 24, 2006).

8. Ibid.

9. "Uniting the world against AIDS: Sub-Saharan Africa," UNAIDS, n.d., <http://www.unaids.org/en/Coordination/Regions/default.asp> (June 25, 2006).

10. "About WHO," World Health Organization, 2005, <http://www.who.int/about/en> (September 30, 2005).

11. "Access to HIV treatment continues to accelerate in developing countries, but bottlenecks persist, says WHO/UNAIDS report," World Health Organization, June 2005, <http://www.who.int/3by5/progressreportJune2005/en/index.html> (September 30, 2005).

12. "HIV/AIDS and Children: UNICEF in Action," UNICEF, n.d.,

<http://www.unicef.org/aids/index_action.html> (September 30, 2005).

13. "HIV/AIDS and Children: The Big Picture," UNICEF, n.d., <http://www.unicef.org/aids/index_bigpicture.html > (September 23, 2006).

14. Emma Guest, *Children of AIDS: Africa's Orphan Crisis* (Sterling, Va.: Pluto Press, 2003), p. 120.

15. "HIV/AIDS and Children: UNICEF in Action."

16. "This Is USAID," U.S. Agency for International Development, January 7, 2005, <http://www.usaid.gov/about_usaid> (September 30, 2005).

17. "About Us," World Bank, 2005, <http://web.worldbank.org/WBSITE/EXTERNAL/EXTABOUTUS/0,,pagePK:50004410~piPK:36602~theSitePK:29708,00.html> (September 30, 2005).

18. Sofia Gruskin and Daniel Tarantola, "Human Rights and HIV/AIDS," *HIV InSite Knowledge Base Chapter,* April 2002, <http://hivinsite.ucsf.edu/InSite?page=kb-08-01-07> (September 27, 2005).

19. Guest, p. 6.

20. Dennis Coday, "To fight AIDS, condoms may be OK," *National Catholic Reporter,* vol. 41, no. 13, January 28, 2005, p. 3.

21. "HIV sex without condom also violates fifth commandment," *America,* vol. 190, no. 3, February 2, 2004, p. 5.

22. "The ABC of HIV Prevention," *Avert.org,* May 10, 2006, <http://www.avert.org/abc-hiv.htm> (June 10, 2006).

23. Kavitha Rajagopalan, "Not So Easy as ABC," *InterAction Library,* March 8, 2004, <http://www.interaction.org/library/detail.php?id=2748> (September 30, 2005).

24. Cynthia Dailard, "Understanding 'Abstinence': Implications for Individuals, Programs and Policies," *The Guttmacher Report on Public Policy* (New York: The Alan Guttmacher Institute, December 2003), p. 5.

25. Rajagopalan.

26. "Beyond Slogans: Lessons from Uganda's ABC Experience," *The Guttmacher Report on Public Policy* (New York: The Alan Guttmacher Institute, December 2003), pp. 1–3.

27. Ibid.

28. "Hollywood Brings Message of Hope for Africa to Heartland with ONE Campaign; World Premiere on AOL; Viewpoint Campaign to Reach Millions," *U.S. Newswire*, March 1, 2006, <http://releases.usnewswire.com/GetRelease.asp?id=61641> (June 27, 2006).

29. Dailard, p. 6.

30. "Is it churlish to criticise Bush over his spending on aids?" editorial, *The Lancet*, vol. 364, no. 9431, July 24, 2004, p. 303.

31. Susan Hunter, *Black Death: AIDS in Africa* (New York: Palgrave MacMillan, 2003), p. 43.

32. Alexander Irwin, Joyce Millen, and Dorothy Fallows, *Global AIDS: Myths and Facts; Tools for Fighting the AIDS Pandemic* (Cambridge, Mass.: South End Press, 2003), pp. 76–77.

33. Hunter, p. 32.

34. Ibid., p. 33

Chapter 9 The United States and the Fight Against AIDS

1. "Funding the fight against AIDS," *Avert.org*, August 23, 2006, <www.avert.org/aidsmoney.htm> (August 25, 2006).

2. "Annual Report to Congress on the President's Emergency Plan for AIDS Relief," U.S. Department of State, Office of the U.S. Global AIDS Coordinator, February 8, 2006, <http://www.state.gov/s/gac/rl/60847.htm> (September 24, 2006).

3. Ibid.

4. Ibid.

5. "Providing drug treatment for millions," *Avert.org*, July 26, 2005, <http://www.avert.org/drugtreatment.htm> (October 2, 2005).

6. "TRIPS, AIDS & generic drugs," *Avert.org*, May 11, 2006, <http://www.avert.org/generic.htm> (June 25, 2006).

7. Heather Boonstra, "U.S. AIDS Policy: Priority on Treatment,

Conservatives' Approach to Prevention," *The Guttmacher Report on Public Policy* (New York: The Alan Guttmacher Institute, August 2003), p. 3.

8. Ibid.

9. Susan A. Cohen, "Beyond Slogans: Lessons from Uganda's ABC Experience," *The Guttmacher Report on Public Policy*, December 2003, vol. 6, no. 5, <http://www.guttmacher.org/pubs/tgr/06/5/gr060501.html> (September 24, 2006).

10. Boonstra, p. 2.

11. "Funding the fight against AIDS."

12. Greg Behrman, *The Invisible People: How the U.S. Has Slept Through the Global AIDS Pandemic, the Greatest Humanitarian Catastrophe of Our Time* (New York: Free Press, 2004), pp. xi–xiv.

13. Alexander Irwin, Joyce Millen, and Dorothy Fallows, *Global AIDS: Myths and Facts; Tools for Fighting the AIDS Pandemic* (Cambridge, Mass.: South End Press, 2003), p. 169.

14. "Is it churlish to criticise Bush over his spending on aids?" editorial, *The Lancet*, vol. 364, no. 9431, July 24, 2004, p. 303.

15. "About Us," Oxfam International, 2006, <http://www.oxfam.org/en/about/> (June 24, 2006).

16. "False hope or new start? The Global Fund to Fight HIV/AIDS, TB, and Malaria," Oxfam International, 24 Oxfam Briefing Paper, p. 4, May 8, 2006, <http://www.oxfam.org/en/files/pp0206_false_hope_or_new_start.pdf> (June 24, 2006).

17. Susan Hunter, *Black Death: AIDS in Africa* (New York: Palgrave MacMillan, 2003), p. 33.

18. "Survey of G7 Nations on HIV Spending in Developing Countries," The Kaiser Family Foundation, July 2005, <http://www.kff.org/hivaids/upload/Survey-of-G7-Nations-on-HIV-Spending-in-Developing-Countries-Survey-Toplines.pdf> (June 27, 2006).

19. Ibid.

20. "False hope or new start? The Global Fund to Fight HIV/AIDS, TB, and Malaria," p. 13.

21. "Then and Now: Magic Johnson," *CNN.com*, June 22, 2005, <http://www.cnn.com/2005/US/01/17/cnn25.tan.johnson/index.html> (June 27, 2006).

22. Ibid.

23. Irwin, Millen, and Fallows, p. 157.

24. Ibid., pp. 162–163.

25. Ibid., p. 165.

26. Behrman, p. xiv.

27. "A Look at the U.S. Global AIDS Policy," *The Guttmacher Report on Public Policy* (New York: The Alan Guttmacher Institute, August 2003), p. 3.

28. "United Nations Universal Declaration of Human Rights, 1948–1998," United Nations, December 10, 1948, <http://www.un.org/Overview/rights.html> (October 1, 2005).

29. Sofia Gruskin and Daniel Tarantola, "Human Rights and HIV/AIDS," *HIV InSite Knowledge Base Chapter*, April 2002, <http://hivinsite.ucsf.edu/InSite?page=kb-08-01-07> (September 27, 2005).

30. Ibid.

31. Ibid.

Chapter 10 The Future of AIDS

1. "AIDS spreading faster than efforts to stop it—But U.N. report finds encouraging signs amid growing epidemic," *MSNBC.com*, June 2, 2005, <http://www.msnbc.msn.com/id/8072321> (June 2, 2005).

Glossary

ABC Program—Program used in Uganda and elsewhere that promotes HIV prevention through Abstinence, Being faithful, and using Condoms, in that order. The U.S. government supports this program.

abstinence—Avoiding sexual contact or intercourse. Promoted by some as the only way to prevent HIV transmission; however, the definition can be confusing. Some define it as avoiding all sexual contact, including oral sex, while some define it as avoiding intercourse.

AIDS (acquired immunodeficiency syndrome)—A severe immunological disorder caused by the retrovirus HIV. There is no cure and it leads to death, usually from opportunistic infections.

antibody—A protein molecule created by the immune system in response to an antigen. This starts a process to fight foreign invaders, such as viruses. Some antibodies attach themselves to antigens. This marks the antigen for destruction by other immune system cells.

antigen—Any substance that causes the body to create antibodies.

antiretroviral—A type of drug used to fight retroviral infections.

Centers for Disease Control and Prevention (CDC)—One of the thirteen major operating components of the U.S. Department of Health and Human Services. It protects the health and safety of all Americans and provides essential human services, especially for those people who are least able to help themselves.

condom—A barrier, usually made of latex or rubber, to cover the penis during sexual intercourse to prevent pregnancy or sexually transmitted diseases. Female condoms are also available.

discrimination—Treatment of another person based on class or category rather than individual merit. It is often a reaction to race, ethnicity, religion, gender, age, or sexual preference.

epidemic—An outbreak of a contagious disease that spreads rapidly and widely.

epidemiology—The study of infectious diseases, including their origins and how they spread.

Global Fund—The Global Fund to Fight AIDS, Tuberculosis and Malaria, established to fight these diseases as a partnership between governments, societies, and private sectors.

heterosexuality—Sexual attraction to members of the opposite sex.

HIV (human immunodeficiency virus)—A retrovirus that causes AIDS by infecting helper T cells of the immune system.

homosexuality—Sexual attraction to members of the same sex. Men are often referred to as "gay" and women are referred to as "lesbian."

immune system—The body's system that protects the body from foreign substances, cells, and tissues by producing the immune response. It includes the thymus, spleen, lymph nodes, lymphoid tissue, the B and T cells, and antibodies.

lymphocyte—Cells found in the blood, lymph, and lymphoid tissues, consisting of about 25 percent white blood cells and including B and T cells.

mother-to-child-transmission (MTCT)—The transfer of HIV from a mother to her baby through pregnancy, birth, or breastfeeding.

opportunistic infection—An infection that normally is not fatal but occurs in cases where the immune system is damaged, and then it becomes fatal.

pandemic—An epidemic that covers a large geographic area.

PEPFAR (President's Emergency Plan for AIDS Relief)—President George W. Bush's plan to fight AIDS.

Ryan White CARE Act—Federal legislation that addresses the unmet health needs of persons living with HIV disease. The CARE Act was named after Ryan White. CARE stands for Comprehensive AIDS Resources Emergency.

sexually transmitted disease (STD)—A type of disease that is contracted through sexual intercourse or other intimate sexual contact.

sub-Saharan Africa—The region of Africa south of the Sahara.

T cells—Any of the lymphocytes that mature in the thymus and have the ability to recognize specific peptide antigens through the receptors on their cell surface.

UNICEF—The United Nation's Children's Fund. UNICEF promotes and educates on issues related to children.

United Nations—An international organization composed of most of the countries of the world. It was founded in 1945 to promote peace, security, and economic development.

vaccine—A weakened or inactivated pathogen that stimulates antibody production against the pathogen but will not cause severe infection.

viruses—Very simple parasites that often cause disease. Viruses are unable to replicate without a host cell.

World Bank—A United Nations agency created to assist developing nations by providing low-interest loans and grants.

World Health Organization (WHO)—A United Nations agency that coordinates international health activities and helps governments improve health services.

For More Information

Global Agencies

United Nations
UN Headquarters
First Avenue at 46th Street
New York, NY 10017

World Health Organization
Regional Office for the Americas
525 23rd Street NW
Washington, DC 20037
202-974-3000

The World Bank
1818 H Street NW
Washington, DC 20433 USA
202-473-1000

U.S. Agencies

Centers for Disease Control and Prevention (CDC)
National Center for HIV/AIDS and TB Prevention
1600 Clifton Road
Atlanta, GA 30333
404-639-0900

U.S. Agency for International Development (USAID)
Information Center
Ronald Reagan Building
Washington, DC 20523-1000
202-712-0000

National Institutes for Health (NIH)
9000 Rockville Pike
Bethesda, MD 20892
301-496-4000

Activist Groups

Student Global AIDS Campaign
Global Justice
1225 Connecticut Avenue NW, Suite 401
Washington, DC 20036
202-296-6727

AIDS Treatment News
7985 Santa Monica Blvd. #99
West Hollywood, CA 90046

Further Reading

Brynie, Faith Hickman. *101 Questions About Your Immune System You Felt Defenseless to Answer—Until Now.* Brookfield, Conn.: Twenty-First Century Books, 2000.

Connolly, Sean. *AIDS.* Chicago: Heinemann Library, 2003.

Ellis, Deborah. *Our Stories, Our Songs: African Children Talk About AIDS.* Markham, Ont.: Fitzhenry & Whiteside, 2005.

Farrell, Jeanette. *Invisible Enemies: Stories of Infectious Diseases.* News York: Farrar, Straus, Giroux, 2005.

Howard, Helen. *Living With AIDS: Mary's Story.* Milwaukee, Wisc.: World Almanac Library, 2005.

Reed, Jennifer. *The AIDS Epidemic: Disaster and Survival.* Berkeley Heights, N.J.: Enslow Publishers, 2005.

Watstein, Sarah Barbara, and Stephen E. Stratton. *The Encyclopedia of HIV and AIDS.* New York: Facts on File, 2003.

Whelan, Jo. *AIDS.* Austin, Tex.: Raintree Steck-Vaughn, 2002.

Internet Addresses

AVERT
  <http://www.avert.org>

The United Nations Joint Programme on AIDS
  <http://www.unaids.org>

U.S. Centers for Disease Control and Prevention
  <http://www.cdc.gov>

Index